Pra
The User-Friendly Book of Mormon

"*User-friendly* perfectly describes Marilyn Faulkner's fresh new study guide for the Book of Mormon. Faulkner manages a breakout book that belongs on the top of your reading list. Her clever prose, visual metaphors, and modern parables help us connect the scriptures to the reality of our lives. It not only trumps the best of what's out there in its genre, but it also creates a unique new approach rich enough to be a lesson manual all on its own."

—**Kieth Merrill,** Academy Award–winning
producer and author

"I can't wait to study the Book of Mormon with Marilyn's questions in mind: 'Where am I in this story? Where is Jesus in this story? What is He trying to teach me? How can this story change my life right now?' Has the Book of Mormon ever been applied in a more practical, personal, and friendly way? I doubt it!"

—**Wendy Ulrich,** PhD, MBA, psychologist
and author of *Weakness Is Not a Sin*

"*Relevance* and *personal connections* are buzzwords in today's educational circles. Faulkner has accomplished both by writing about contemporary issues with wit and a good dose of humor. Never sacrificing sacred and deeper meanings, she allows us to enter into the world of Book of Mormon stories through our own portals of understanding and personal need. I found myself chuckling and nodding with recognition at my own follies, foibles, and questions as I read along."

—**Rita Riddle Wright,** PhD,
director of the Springville Arts Museum

THE
USER-FRIENDLY
BOOK *of*
MORMON

THE
USER-FRIENDLY
BOOK *of*
MORMON

TIMELESS
TRUTHS
for TODAY'S
CHALLENGES

MARILYN GREEN
FAULKNER

CFI
An Imprint of Cedar Fort, Inc.
Springville, Utah

ISBN 13: 978-1-4621-1843-4

Published by CFI, an imprint of Cedar Fort, Inc.
2373 W. 700 S., Springville, UT 84663
Distributed by Cedar Fort, Inc., www.cedarfort.com

LIBRARY OF CONGRESS CATALOGING-IN-PUBLICATION DATA

Names: Faulkner, Marilyn Green, 1953- author.
Title: The user-friendly Book of Mormon : timeless truths for today's
  challenges / Marilyn Green Faulkner.
Description: Springville, Utah : CFI, an imprint of Cedar Fort, Inc., [2016]
  | Includes bibliographical references and index. | Description based on
  print version record and CIP data provided by publisher; resource not
  viewed.
Identifiers: LCCN 2016001331 (print) | LCCN 2015050939 (ebook) | ISBN
  9781462126378 (epub, pdf, mobi) | ISBN 9781462118434 (perfect bound : alk.
  paper)
Subjects: LCSH: Book of Mormon--Criticism, interpretation, etc. | Church of
  Jesus Christ of Latter-day Saints--Doctrines. | Mormon Church--Doctrines.
Classification: LCC BX8627 (print) | LCC BX8627 .F38 2016 (ebook) | DDC
  289.3/22--dc23
LC record available at http://lccn.loc.gov/2016001331

Cover design by Shawnda T. Craig
Cover design © 2016 Cedar Fort, Inc.
Edited and typeset by Kevin Haws

Printed in the United States of America

10 9 8 7 6 5 4 3 2 1

Printed on acid-free paper

Dedicated with love to Craig, our children, and our grandchildren.

*"And as I partook of the fruit thereof it filled my soul
with exceedingly great joy; wherefore, I began to be
desirous that my family should partake of it also; for I knew
that it was desirable above all other fruit"* (1 Nephi 8:12).

Contents

Contents

Contents

Preface: Why the Book of Mormon Is Worth Studying, Even If You're Not a Mormon

When Joseph Smith published the Book of Mormon in 1830, he made some pretty fantastic claims about its divine origin. Wikipedia sums it up for us:

> The Book of Mormon is a sacred text of the Latter-day Saint movement, which adherents believe contains writings of ancient prophets who lived on the American continent from approximately 2200 BC to AD 421. It was first published in March 1830 by Joseph Smith as *The Book of Mormon: An Account Written by the Hand of Mormon upon Plates Taken from the Plates of Nephi.*
>
> According to Smith's account and the book's narrative, the Book of Mormon was originally written in otherwise unknown characters referred to as "reformed Egyptian" engraved on golden plates. Smith said that the last prophet to contribute to the book, a man named Moroni, buried it in a hill in present-day New York, then returned to earth in 1827 as an angel, revealing the location of the book to Smith, and instructing him to translate it into English for use in the restoration of Christ's true Church in the latter days. . . . [The Book of Mormon] has since been fully or partially translated into 108 languages. As of 2011, more than 150 million copies of the Book of Mormon have been published.[1]

Preface

Why Should Non-Mormons Read the Book of Mormon?

Though the recent Broadway play made the Book of Mormon a household name, as a sacred text it is largely ignored outside of the Church, except by some few who have devoted themselves to debunking it. As Terryl Givens said, "What the Book of Mormon claims to be is so radical that the storms of controversy over its origins and authenticity have almost completely obscured the text itself."[2] Some Christians feel that it is heretical to believe that anything could be added to the Bible—thus reading the Book of Mormon represents a kind of blasphemy. Others find the book's premise of a Hebrew population immigrating to the American continent unsupportable by historical evidence. And most find the idea that a young man in New York could have translated a record engraved on golden plates too outlandish to be taken seriously.

So why bother with the Book of Mormon at all? Here are three reasons to take a look:

It will help you understand the Mormons in your life. There are currently about fifteen million members of The Church of Jesus Christ of Latter-day Saints worldwide, so the chances are good that you have a friend or a relative who regularly reads the Book of Mormon. If so, becoming acquainted with this scripture can lead to a greater understanding of someone you love. Grant Hardy, who teaches a course on the sacred literatures of the world, contended that to understand another person, it is important to understand his or her beliefs. "There appears to be a significant spiritual component to being human, as we might expect from our understanding that all people are children of God. . . . Showing respect for and knowing the basic beliefs of major religious traditions is an important part of being a global citizen."[3]

Every sacred text has something to teach us. You don't have to believe in the divine origin of the Book of Mormon to find many things in the text that are inspiring and uplifting and that expand your understanding of spiritual things. Krister Stendahl, the former dean of the Harvard Divinity School and Bishop of Stockholm in the Church of Sweden, urged people to leave room for "holy envy"; that is, leave room for finding beauty and meaning in religious practices or beliefs that are not part of their own religious training.[4]

I have found this to be true. I've been moved to tears in a Jewish synagogue as worshippers kissed their fingers and reverently touched the Torah scroll, causing me to appreciate more fully the importance of scripture. The devout expressions of Buddhist monks in prayer and the humble genuflection of Catholics as they approach an altar have taught me to be a more reverent Latter-day Saint. In the same way, your faith life can be strengthened by something in this text if you open yourself to it.

There might be something to its claims. The Book of Mormon is unique in its invitation to all readers to "ask God, the Eternal Father, in the name of Christ, if these things are . . . true" (Moroni 10:4). Mormons have a personal concept of revelation, believing that God actually speaks to people through the Spirit. Missionaries are young and usually have just a rudimentary knowledge of our theology, yet they are trusted to represent the LDS faith to others. This is because they are simply instructed to invite every investigator of the Church to read the Book of Mormon and pray *for themselves* about its concepts. This reliance on a heavenly confirmation—rather than an extensive course of religious training—offers an open-ended invitation to any reader of the Book of Mormon. Rather than going through a lengthy course of study, you can just read it, pray about it, and see how you feel.

It's Better to Read It than to Read about It

In any case, you'll never really understand the Book of Mormon unless you actually pick it up and read it. Thomas O'Dea, a Catholic scholar of Mormonism, wryly commented: "The Book of Mormon has not been universally considered by its critics as one of those books that must be read in order to have an opinion of it."[5] Nearly all people have read at least a portion of the Bible and thus are entitled to an opinion about its veracity and value. We would never consider reading an article about the Bible as a basis for forming an opinion on it. The same should be true of the Book of Mormon, yet most people who criticize it have not actually read it.

My purpose is not to argue the historicity or the authenticity of the Book of Mormon. Instead, I wish to make it a little bit easier for interested people to read it and get something useful out of it. In this book, we will examine the Book of Mormon as a work of literature as well as a book of scripture and try to mine from it some of the nuggets of wisdom that have made it precious and important as a sacred text to millions of people, including me.

After all, even that ubiquitous guide to everything, Wikipedia, admits that there are some interesting things in the Book of Mormon and identifies what is, for all Latter-day Saints, the most important message of the book: "The Book of Mormon has a number of original and distinctive doctrinal discussions on subjects such as the fall of Adam and Eve, the nature of the Atonement, eschatology, redemption from physical and spiritual death, and the organization of the latter-day Church. The pivotal event of the book is an appearance of Jesus Christ in the Americas shortly after his resurrection."[6]

Use It as a Complement to the Bible

As I have taught a community Bible class over the last few years, I've been continually inspired by the number of beliefs we all have in common as Christians; these commonalities seem so much more important than the doctrinal issues that divide us. I have used the Book of Mormon as a Bible commentary many times in classes and simply invite those who are not of the LDS faith to enjoy the insight offered if it appeals to them and reject it if it doesn't. With this disclaimer, I have never found the use of the Book of Mormon to be a problem. Our sessions have virtually no doctrinal disputation, as we are much more concerned about our own relations to the teachings of Jesus than various points of doctrine. The good Christians that attend this class soon find that they need not fear—it's just a book.

Increasingly, the world is coming to accept that the Book of Mormon (whether you embrace it as divinely inspired or not) stands on its own as a significant work of literature, based on its character development, complex plotting, and remarkable collection of authors, each uniquely different in tone and voice. In addition, I contend that the Book of Mormon also stands as a great work of sacred scripture, based on the remarkable and original views it espouses on a number of topics: human nature, the mission of Christ, the apocalypse, and so on. Along with the Bible, I feel that it merits its own course of study.

As we progress through each of the fifteen books in the Book of Mormon, I hope you will begin to appreciate the tremendous wealth of knowledge and insight (particularly about the role of Jesus Christ in individual lives) that is available in this unique text. Many modern challenges like class warfare and feminism and personality disorders are dealt with in its pages. If you are not a Latter-day Saint and do not accept the Church's claims about the origin of the Book of Mormon, it's my hope that this study will open your mind to its value as a sacred text and will add to your understanding of your own spiritual quest as a result. If you are a Latter-day Saint and accept this as a standard work, I hope that this commentary will enrich your appreciation of its timeliness and relevance to your daily dilemmas.

It's All about Jesus

My ultimate goal in this book is the same as the stated goal of the Book of Mormon itself, which is to act as another witness of Christ. As Mormon (the brilliant editor and redactor of the book) stated in the closing chapters, there is one sure way to judge the value anything that comes into our purview: "For behold, the Spirit of Christ is given to every man, that he may know good from evil; wherefore, I show unto you the way to judge; for every thing which inviteth to do good, and to persuade to believe in Christ, is sent forth by the power and gift of Christ; wherefore ye may know with a perfect knowledge it is of God" (Moroni 7:16).

The Book of Mormon has offered a significant addition to my knowledge and understanding about Jesus Christ, which is the most important information I possess. Anything that adds to that part of my life is welcome and wonderful to me. I'm grateful for what I have learned from its pages, and I'm excited to journey through them with you.

Notes

1. *Wikipedia*, "Book of Mormon."

2. Terryl L. Givens, *The Book of Mormon: A Very Short Introduction* (New York: Oxford University Press, 2009), 4.

3. Grant Hardy, "'Of Their Own Nation and Tongue,' or Why There Are Actually Five Standard LDS Works," *Meridian Magazine*, February 2014, http://ldsmag.com/article-1-13982/.

4. Krister Stendahl reportedly first used this term at a 1985 press conference in Stockholm, Sweden, in response to opposition to the building of a temple there.

5. Thomas O'Dea, as quoted in Terryl L. Givens, *By the Hand of Mormon* (New York: Oxford University Press, 2002), 86.

6. *Wikipedia*, "Book of Mormon."

Introduction: The User-Friendly Book of Mormon

In the last few decades, whether we like it or not, most of us have been obliged to embrace the digital age, and we find ourselves facing a confusing array of devices with their attendant charge cords, pass codes, and *modi operandi*.

These days, in desperation, I search for devices that are labeled "user-friendly." This is a relatively new term, coined to describe complex machines or systems that are readily accessible without special skills or lengthy sets of instructions. In other words, given a little time and patience and a few helpful suggestions (usually from someone at least half my age), I can eventually get the hang of using them.

This has got me thinking about another device without which we can't function properly: the word of God. Are the scriptures "user-friendly"? I would contend that they are, and all of the new technology available to us is making them even more so. But, like my tablet or FitBit, discovering the power of these wonderful tools takes a little time and effort, as well as sometimes the assistance of a friend. So I thought we might sit down together and take a fresh look at our own unique device for living—the Book of Mormon.

Making the Connection

Have you ever given a friend a Book of Mormon, only to find out that he or she experienced some confusion about what it is? Instead of a book that explains Latter-day Saint beliefs, it turns out to be a narrative about Hebrew emigrants to North America in 600 BC. Let's be honest: though we are familiar with the story and its characters, Latter-day Saints may have a little of the same disconnect in understanding how the Book of Mormon relates to our daily lives. There is a crucial difference between *reading* the scriptures and *using* them.

Let me illustrate. If you're anything like me, this morning you woke up with a set of things on your mind about which you're alternately worrying, praying, or talking on the phone with your friends. We all have sorrows and weaknesses that weigh us down. We wrestle with money concerns and conflicting demands on our time. Our challenges may include health issues, struggling children, addictions, aging parents, marital difficulties, or loneliness. We may be dealing with any of the above and more, because life is difficult by definition. Unfortunately, it is possible that we dutifully study the scriptures without really making a connection between the words and our own lives and struggles. Can we really use the Book of Mormon to address the modern problems that beset us every day?

I believe we can, and as we learn to do so, this book will become user-friendly in the best sense. Rather than a chore on our to-do list, the Book of Mormon can become the blueprint for a Christian life. The key to "liken[ing] all scriptures unto [ourselves]" (1 Nephi 19:23) is to identify the equivalent of our modern problems to the ancient people's own. For example:

- Nephi and his brothers can teach us a lot about family violence.
- Lehi and Sariah can show us how major changes in lifestyle can cause stress on a marriage.
- Alma the Elder and the Younger can illustrate the difference between control and influence in parenting.
- The brother of Jared can teach us about dating. (Really!)
- Mormon can guide us in creating a family history.

These are just a few of the issues we will explore together. The good news is that you don't have to be a scholar to understand the Book of Mormon, nor do you have to understand all of the history or even remember all the names. All you need to get more out of the Book of Mormon is a place to take notes, some quiet time each day, and a commitment to really pay attention. As you read, ask yourself the following questions: Where am I in this story? How does this story relate to me? Where is Jesus in this story, and what is He trying to teach me here? Why is this story in the scriptures at all? And (the most important question) how can this story change my life for the better right now?

Therefore, What?

Elder Jeffrey R. Holland shared this fascinating insight:

President Boyd K. Packer, himself a master teacher and long-time administrator in the Church Educational System, has a question he often asks when we have made a presentation or given some sort of exhortation to one another in the Twelve. He looks up as if to say, "Are you through?" And then says to the speaker (and, by implication, to the rest of the group), "Therefore, what?"

"Therefore, what?" I think that is what the Savior answered day in and day out as an inseparable element of His teaching and preaching. . . . These sermons and exhortations were to no avail if the actual lives of His disciples did not change.[1]

Above all, the scriptures are meant to change us, and the only real key to change is through making a personal connection, both to the story and to the Savior. So as you read, record your thoughts on how these stories relate to you, and then write down everything the story teaches you about Jesus Christ, the Atonement, and His relationship with you. If you do so, your reading of the Book of Mormon will become a source of living water. You'll find yourself really using what you read in your daily life, and the scriptures will become what one artist has called "the antidote for the emptiness of existence."[2] You'll feast upon the wisdom, inspiration, and Christian joy that the Book of Mormon offers. Making the connection between the written word and our own lives is what I think Alma meant when he said, "If ye will nourish the word . . . by your faith with great diligence . . . it shall take root; and behold it shall be a tree springing up unto everlasting life. And because of your diligence and your faith and your patience with the word in nourishing it, that it may take root in you, behold, by and by ye shall pluck the fruit thereof . . . and ye shall feast upon this fruit even until ye are filled, that ye hunger not, neither shall ye thirst" (Alma 32:41–42).

It's Much More User-Friendly with a Friend

Many years ago, a friend of mine joined the Church but struggled to understand the Book of Mormon. We did not live close to each other, so I took a copy of the Book of Mormon and read it with her in mind. I underlined many of my favorite passages and wrote lots of thoughts and questions in the margins, as if we were sitting and reading it together. I then sent the book to her, and she found that it increased her understanding and enjoyment of the text. It turned out to be a wonderful experience for both of us.

Essentially, that is what I've done here. I have gone through the Book of Mormon with you in mind, stopping to talk about passages that have been especially meaningful to me over several decades of reading. Since I'm trained as a student of literature, I'll talk with you about it as a great book, noting the themes, characters, and literary devices that I find especially interesting. For example, I am completely fascinated by the multilayered narration—the original narrator (such as Nephi or Alma) is first edited and redacted by Mormon, and then is funneled through the brilliant yet unlettered mind of Joseph Smith. I love the tone—tragic (yet hopeful), passionate, prophetic, and personal. Since I'm also a wife, mother, and grandmother, I tend to notice the family issues that are so prevalent. I'm also intrigued by the overt Christology of the book, and how its central message of the mission of Jesus Christ informs every story. And finally, I find that the stories themselves have value not just as historical facts but also as parables that can apply to our lives.

This is not a conventional study guide; we won't go verse by verse. We will just hop, skip, and jump through the book, stopping at places that you might find interesting, and then moving on. I hope you'll feel by the end that you have a different perspective on this text and that you'll have the desire and confidence to create your own commentary on this book as it applies to your life. (At the end of each book, I've provided some note pages for you to do just that.) It would be wonderful if you then felt inclined to sit with someone you love (either in person or in writing) and help make the Book of Mormon more user-friendly for him or her.

If You Never Ask Questions, You'll Never Get Answers

As you read, I encourage you to write down your questions. You don't need to feel bad if you have doubts and concerns about what you read; there is no question that you shouldn't ask. Recently, I had a conversation with a woman whose son was undergoing a crisis of faith about Joseph Smith and the Book of Mormon. A leading historian in the Church invited this young man to lunch and listened to all of his concerns about the origins of our faith. At the end, he said, "I have only two words of advice for you in relation to all of this: dig deeper." Rather than encouraging him to avoid thinking about the thorny issues, he encouraged the young man to go a layer further.

That is the best advice I've heard on the subject, and I've certainly found this to be the answer in my study of the Book of Mormon. At first glance, the Book of Mormon may seem to be a confusing conglomeration of plot lines and story fragments, created by an author who was adopting the scriptural tone of the Bible. But as we go deeply into the text together, there is so much more. There is so much that is startling in its originality and so many moments of pure inspiration, that one can come away with a feeling of gratitude for the light and truth that shines through so many of the passages in this book.

So let your preconceived notions slip away, and let's take a look at a great book.

Notes

1. Jeffrey R. Holland, "Therefore, What?" *Teaching Seminary Preservice Readings Religion 370, 471, and 475* (2004), 83.

2. *Midnight in Paris*, directed by Woody Allen (2011).

1 Nephi: The Story of a Civilization Is the Story of One Family

There Goes the Neighborhood: Setting the Scene (1 Nephi 1)

The first book of Nephi takes place during the tumultuous time around the destruction of Jerusalem in 586 BC. This is when the prophet Jeremiah was preaching in Jerusalem, so we can tie the narrative to a verifiable time in history, as recorded in 1 and 2 Chronicles and the book of Jeremiah. From these and other sources, we can get a pretty good idea of what Jerusalem was like when Lehi and Sariah raised their four sons there.

Jerusalem in 600 BC was a civilization in flux. First mentioned in the Bible in connection with Melchizedek (Genesis 14), Jerusalem was revered as the site of Mount Moriah, where Abraham offered Isaac as a sacrifice. For centuries, it was a small city set on about twelve acres, which then doubled in size when Solomon built the temple in 928 BC. By the reign of Hezekiah in 700 BC, the population had swelled to twenty-five thousand because of the thousands who sought refuge there against the advance of the Assyrians from the north.

The Jerusalem that Lehi and Sariah knew covered 125 acres of land and was sandwiched between the competing superpowers of that time—Egypt and Babylon, as well as remnants of former conquerors such as the Assyrians, Medes, and Philistines. Thus, the place in which Lehi and Sariah raised their family was perhaps even more culturally diverse than the Jerusalem of today, and all of the other cultures subscribed to a polytheistic, nature-based theology. In some ways, this would've been attractive to the mainly agrarian population, even though pagan methods of worship could involve sexual deviancy and human sacrifice. There was something immediate and accessible about these gods that the unknowable Yahweh did not offer. In addition, these polytheistic faiths demanded only that their various gods be appeased by performing certain rituals, not the human character being changed and sanctified by obedience to a long list of commandments.[1]

That Lehi and Sariah managed, in the midst of such confusion, to convert any of their children to their strict, monotheistic belief system is a tribute to them. The competing philosophies around them were appealing, as shown by the reactions of their two oldest sons, Laman and Lemuel. They considered their father's revelations to be hallucinations and had one main desire after the family left the city: to get out of the wilderness and back to their comfortable home in Jerusalem.

A Visionary Man Sets the Tone

Nephi recorded that in the first year of the reign of Zedekiah (600 BC), a number of prophets began prophesying about the impending destruction of Jerusalem. Lehi was greatly moved by this and "prayed unto the Lord, yea, even with all his heart, in behalf of his people" (1 Nephi 1:5). Whether Lehi had an ecclesiastical calling at this time, we are not told. Nephi then wrote of six visions given to Lehi in fairly quick succession.

Every great work of literature features themes that give it cohesiveness, and the Book of Mormon has several that are introduced through these six visions. There are three that particularly stand out for me: the eternal nature of the family, the mission of Jesus Christ, and the multifaceted nature of divine revelation.

Theme 1: The Eternal Family

Beginning with its opening words of the first chapter, "I, Nephi, having been born of goodly parents," the Book of Mormon identifies itself as a family drama. Its stories revolve around husbands and wives, fathers and sons, and brothers and sisters. This is one of the characteristics of the narrative that makes it so relatable in any age. Along with revelations about Christ and the plan of salvation, we also see Lehi receiving a personal vision directing him to find wives for his sons and create the nexus for a new civilization. Though the narrative will bounce back and forth between the public and private issues in this way, it is always centered on the family.

The Book of Mormon shows us a variety of families dealing with the same problems we face every day. Once we get rid of the idea that there is only one way to be righteous, we can freely examine their different approaches to parenting, their involvement in politics, their marital challenges, and the family conflicts. Looking to their examples, we can draw insights about our own lives as a result.

Theme 2: The Mission of Jesus Christ

Lehi was "carried away in a vision" (1 Nephi 1:18) that featured similar components to the "call visions" of Jeremiah, Isaiah, and Moses: he saw God on His throne, surrounded by angels.

However, at this point, there is a sharp departure from parallel visions recorded in the Old Testament. Lehi saw "one descending out of the midst of heaven," followed by twelve disciples (1 Nephi 1:9). This is the first of countless specific references to Jesus Christ in the Book of Mormon. The mission of Christ, His Atonement and all of its ramifications, occupies most of the doctrinal commentary in the book.

If you have any doubt about the Christo-centricity of the Book of Mormon, take a highlighter and mark every passage that either refers to or teaches something about Jesus Christ; it's a pretty impressive exercise. Jesus Christ is mentioned by name in the book hundreds of years before His birth. The law of Moses was lived as a precursor to His coming, and many sermons were preached about His mission long before He came.

Theme 3: Personal Revelation

The fact that the Book of Mormon opens with a report of Lehi's six visions suggests something important about the book: a firm belief in a personal God who speaks to His children. The nature of revelation—how it is given and received (and even how much negotiation is allowed on the part of the recipient)—is often addressed in the stories.

After receiving death threats in response to his preaching, Lehi was commanded in a dream to "take his family and depart into the wilderness" (1 Nephi 2:1). This introduces another facet of the revelation theme: the wilderness as a place where God may be found. From the Old Testament to Shakespeare to the Lord of the Rings series, the wilderness is used as a setting for making contact with the divine. As our scriptural characters go into the wilderness, we leave our own spiritual comfort zones and travel with them. Then, as we encounter wilderness moments in our lives, we turn to their experiences, and they travel with us. Either way, we aren't alone.

Finally, divine revelation is a two-way process. The sixth and final vision of the tree of life serves to introduce the ways that people respond to divine direction. This theme will recur in myriad ways until the closing words of the book, which issues a personal challenge to every reader to "ask God . . . in the name of Christ, if these things are not true" (Moroni 10:4). Thus the opening theme—God revealing His will to mankind—is bookended by the closing concept that revelation is a two-way process. God speaks but can only be heard if people choose to receive and believe.

1 Nephi: A Parabolic Overture

In their book *The First Christmas*, scholars Marcus Borg and John Dominic Crossan described each of the birth narratives of Jesus (Matthew 1–2 and Luke 1–2) as a "parabolic overture" to the Gospel that follows.[2] Just to unpack that phrase, an overture is the orchestral piece that comes at the beginning of a production and offers a preview of what to expect from the whole work. A parable is a simple but highly symbolic story that communicates a specific moral or message.

The authors asserted that Matthew's objective in his Gospel can be previewed by examining how His birth stories (Herod's role, the Magi, Joseph's dreams, and so on) point to Christ's role as the King of the Jews, the second Moses, and the Giver of the New Law. Luke's stories (the stable, shepherds, manger, and so on) emphasize the humble nature of Christ's birth, foreshadowing Luke's portrayal of Christ's mission to the marginalized and the oppressed.

This fascinating insight can be applied to the Book of Mormon as well and perhaps helps explain why so much attention is given in 1 Nephi to the dissension in Lehi's family. The elements in 1 Nephi, beginning with a prophetic vision that leads both to the salvation and the destruction of a family is a fitting overture to the entire book. The story of Lehi's family, both tragic and triumphant, can be viewed as a parable of what will happen to a civilization. At its center is Nephi's great vision of the Savior and His mission, foreshadowing the central event of the book—the appearance of Christ to the Nephites.

The Parable of Nephi and Netflix (1 Nephi 4)

Scriptural characters have an added dimension—their life experiences are typological; they help elucidate larger truths. Abraham and Isaac aren't just a father and son; they represent *the* Father and *the* Son. Moses isn't just a baby hidden in a basket who grows up to save a nation; he represents the promised Redeemer, born in obscurity and destined to save mankind. The things that happen to scriptural characters aren't just for them; their life experience can be interpreted typologically, pointing to Christ. Jesus employed typology often during His ministry, most memorably on the road to Emmaus after His Resurrection, where "beginning at Moses and all the prophets, he expounded unto them in all the scriptures the things concerning himself" (Luke 24:27).

On another level, the experiences of scriptural characters can be used as 'types' to understand our own life experiences. In this sense, they are parabolic in nature.

Nephi is not just a young man sent on an errand; he represents each of us when faced by a seemingly insurmountable challenge. One way to "liken all scriptures" (1 Nephi 19:23) to ourselves is to assign a symbolic meaning to each component of the story. As we read, we might ask ourselves, "Is there something about this story that stands for something in my own life? Can I read this as a parable?" Let's try it.

The story of Nephi going back to Jerusalem to get the brass plates is inspiring on the surface because of his faith and courage. But it also lends itself to interpretation as a parable.

If I am Nephi trying to bring the scriptures into my life, who or what might my Laban be? Who or what do I have to "kill" to make the scriptures mine? My "Laban" may be too much TV, time at the gym, or work. My "Laban" may be too much socializing and not enough personal time. Whatever is keeping me from the scriptures must be eliminated.

To be victorious over the adversary, we may need to take the Sword of Laban and cut the cable cord. The moral of the story? It is better that one Netflix series go unwatched than a whole soul perish in unbelief!

Lehi's Dream: Only God Can Make a Tree of Life (1 Nephi 8)

Just a few chapters into the Book of Mormon, we find ourselves in the middle of an allegory—an extended symbolic journey filled with dark mists, a great and spacious building, and a glorious tree with shining fruit. Just what does it all mean? In fact, we might well ask, Why is spiritual information so often conveyed to us through symbols? After all, if the scriptures are so important for our eternal welfare, why make them so obscure and difficult to understand? Why not just tell us what we need to know without all the poetic, flowery language?

To address this question, we need to take a moment and think about language, because the scriptures are made of words. All words are representative by nature; they consist of sets of letters that, when grouped together, stand for something in our world. But certain words take on a double meaning and become symbols. This means that they stand for real objects (like trees and seeds) but may also be used to help us understand more abstract, immaterial concepts (like love and faith.) Because scriptures attempt to explain the most abstract concepts, they abound with symbolic language. And precisely because these multilayered words require more mental work, the scriptures have the power to impact us more deeply.

How does symbolic language help us understand spiritual things? To begin with, it wakes up the brain. For example, in the Bible when Jesus said that your faith need only be the size of a mustard seed, an interesting thing happens in your brain. To help you arrive at an understanding of this statement, the side of your brain that collects data fires off whatever it has on file about mustard seeds (that they are tiny, for example). In response, the side that has some understanding of the concept of faith, including the emotive content of that word, sends a message or two (such as faith is believing but not knowing, I feel unsure about many spiritual things, and so on).

Combining two things that normally don't occur together causes an immediate reaction: the two sides of the brain must communicate in order to grasp the meaning. This connection is called a synapse. Each synapse—the electrical connection between the two sides of the brain—creates a tiny physical change that may be compared to adding a groove to an old record album. When synapses fire, the brain actually grows. As a result of that connection, we are able to go from just collecting facts or feeling vague emotions to *understanding*. I believe that just as the physical mind grows when symbols are introduced to it, the spiritual mind grows when symbols are contemplated over time.

What's in a Tree?

Lehi's vision centers around one of the most ubiquitous symbols in all of scripture—the tree of life. Found at the center of Eden (both literally and figuratively), the tree of life turns up in various iterations throughout the canon, including but not limited to the tree in Eden, the allegorical olive tree that represents a variety of concepts, including the house of Israel and the Atonement of Christ, the healing staff Moses raised in the wilderness, the cross of Crucifixion, and Alma's seed of faith that, when planted in the heart, grows into a tree of life inside each of us.

Real, physical trees help us to make a connection between gospel principles and our own life experiences. We can contemplate the characteristics of a tree that relate to faith (seeds), testimony (fruit), and the firm foundation we have in Jesus (roots) to understand the meaning of these abstract concepts. So as we learn to appreciate the symbolic language in the scriptures, we begin to understand them more deeply. Our brains and our souls grow a little.

The scriptures are difficult to read, but they are so for a good reason. Like Jacob in conflict with the angel, our mental and spiritual muscles grow as we wrestle with the scriptures. We might view it as a workout that will be difficult but will also produce a sense of accomplishment and even euphoria after finishing. We learn new things all the time in life—why not in scripture study? If we can learn to type with our fingers and use Skype, then we can master the subtleties of symbols.

Look! A Case Study in the Condescension of God (1 Nephi 11)

How does the symbolic language of Lehi's vision connect to our daily lives? Nephi had essentially the same question, and his experience can teach us something about the purpose of scripture stories. Nephi began by seeking to *understand* the visions that his father had, but it turns out that the Spirit of the Lord may have a different definition of that word. What does it mean to understand the scriptures? Perhaps, rather than accumulating data about the doctrines, *understanding* may refer more to the literal interpretation of the word: to stand under the truth as it pours out upon one in a life-changing deluge of living water. The key that unlocks that floodgate is often a symbol.

Most of us have had a moment when the abstract, archaic words of scripture have suddenly become present and personal. The conversation between Nephi and the Spirit of the Lord has been precious to me since a cold snowy day over forty years ago, when the symbolic language of the narrative all came together and opened my mind and heart.

I was sitting in our old Volvo, waiting for my brother to finish an errand. I had my Book of Mormon with me and was reading 1 Nephi 11, in which Nephi prayed to understand the vision of his father and got a little more than he bargained for. As I had done many times, I read the interview between the Spirit of the Lord and Nephi and marveled at the way the Lord handled this teaching moments. When Nephi asked about the meaning of the tree of life, he probably expected a doctrinal discourse. Instead, the Spirit simply said, "Look!" (1 Nephi 11:12). Then Nephi was shown Mary, holding Jesus in her arms. The word *look* is repeated so many times in the chapter that it got my attention. The other word that caught my attention was *behold*. It was a word that seemed to describe a dimension beyond just looking.

For the first time, I noticed that the words used to describe Mary were exactly the same as those used to describe the fruit and the tree in Lehi's dream (white, pure, and so on). This interested me, and I kept flipping back and forth, seeing how the same words were used in Lehi's description of the tree and Nephi's description of the virgin. White, fair, and pure. And she was *bearing* (not holding) the child in her arms.

This use of language seemed to connect Mary to both the tree and to the fruit. *Well,* I thought, *is Mary the tree? Is Jesus the tree, the fruit, or both?* Without realizing it, I had moved into the position of Nephi, asking the Spirit of the Lord for the meaning of the vision. This happened because the metaphorical language was causing synapses to fire; my brain was engaged, and I was curious to know what it all meant. In addition, the vision of Mary and Jesus spoke to my womanly heart. I was touched that of all of the ways the Lord could use to talk about His love, this was the image He chose.

Gradually, the interconnecting words became a scene in my mind, and my heart began to pound. For just a moment, it was as if I could behold Mary, holding Jesus in her arms, and Nephi, beholding her, and the Lord, beholding them beholding Him. The tree of life, the love of God, Mary bearing the child—it all came together. I can still remember that moment, sitting in the cold car and holding the book tight in my shaking hands. I felt right down to my toes that the whole meaning of the story, of the scriptures, and of life itself was encompassed in the image of that mother holding that baby; the baby who would be slain from before the foundation of the world and was willing to come down to earth and be born in a stable so that no human being would ever be alone.

Suddenly, all of the worries I had about school, dating, and an uncertain future seemed manageable. I wasn't alone! Jesus had experienced everything I would ever face and more. He loved me and knew me. His willingness to descend with me was infinite, so I really had nothing to fear. From that moment on, I have never thought about Nephi's vision without feeling that personal, grateful, worshipful connection to the Savior that I felt then. The little change in my heart that day has stayed with me, and it all started with some rich symbolic language.

Chiasmus in the Book of Mormon

Quite a lot has been written about the use of chiasmus in the Book of Mormon. Chiasmus is a literary structure that became generally noticed by scholars in the early 1900s and is now recognized as a hallmark of Hebrew poetry. Simply explained, in a chiastic structure everything is said twice, and in the repetition every statement is made in inverse order, so that the statements form a "V." The most important point in the verse or the chapter will be found at the center of the passage. Here's a simple example from Psalm 3:7–8 which reads, "Arise, O Lord; save me, O my God: for thou hast smitten all mine enemies upon the cheek bone; thou hast broken the teeth of the ungodly. Salvation belongeth unto the Lord: thy blessing is upon thy people."

Here are the way the components line up:

a save me
  b O my God
    c for thou hast smitten
      d all mine enemies
        e upon the cheek bone
        e the teeth
      d of the ungodly
    c thou hast broken
  b the Lord
a salvation

Several years ago, LDS scholar John Welch discovered the extensive use of this uniquely Hebrew poetic structure in the Book of Mormon. The following is his summary of its importance:

> Taken as evidence of the Book of Mormon, chiasmus offers us a touchstone like we have rarely ever had before. Scholars are saying things today like, "Where there is chiasmus, there is the influence of a Hebraic hand." And yet such a thing was totally unknown to Joseph Smith and universally unrecognized by the world until the present decade. While the Book of Mormon is richly chiastic, extensive structural chiasmus has yet to be found in any other literature in the world other than the Hebrew. Thus it seems that we are able to meet the demands of an exceptionally strong conditional here: Chiasmus is in a literature *if* and *only if* its roots are Hebraic.[3]

Not only is chiasmus found in individual verses, but it is also found in several of the most important chapters in the Book of Mormon. Alma 36 is a beautiful example.[4] Perhaps most remarkable of all is the fact that entire books, including 1 Nephi and the book of Mosiah, are also constructed in this way.[5]

A Parable: Tripping Over the Liahona (1 Nephi 16)

One day when Lehi looked out of the tent door, there was something new. As he "arose in the morning, and went forth to the tent door, to his great astonishment he beheld upon the ground a round ball of curious workmanship; and it was of fine brass. And within the ball were two spindles; and the one pointed the way whither we should go into the wilderness" (1 Nephi 16:10).

For a family lost in the wilderness, nothing could be more welcome than a compass. But this was a different kind of compass; it only worked under certain conditions: "The pointers which were in the ball . . . did work according to the faith and diligence and heed which we did give unto them. And there was also written upon them a new writing, which was plain to be read, which did give us understanding concerning the ways of the Lord; and it was written and changed from time to time, according to the faith and diligence which we gave unto it" (1 Nephi 16:28–29).

How Can I Get One of These?

If thousands of people line up for each new version of the iPhone, imagine what a response a device like the Liahona would generate! What in our lives today is like the Liahona? Well, because it acted as a guide for Lehi and his family and was only activated by faith and actually contained words of guidance, the Liahona could symbolize the word of God in our lives. Or perhaps because it was something special and outside the day-to-day routine and was a little hard to understand, it might symbolize the temple. In either case, we have in the Liahona a symbolic source of divine guidance that is close at hand yet requires significant spiritual preparation to utilize.

Is there a "Liahona" waiting at the door of your tent? Are you stepping over it every morning rather than taking time to consult it? Taking a few minutes to read the scriptures or to attend a temple session doesn't get noted anywhere. We don't get credit or praise for it, nor can we deduct it from our tithing. But these quiet efforts to get in touch with God's guidance can make a significant difference. They help us to align our lives with the spiritual promptings of the Holy Ghost and with the celestial course laid before us.

Just Slightly Off Course Can Be Deadly

President Dieter F. Uchtdorf compared being in tune with spiritual guidance to the navigation of a great airliner. In his talk, he described the true story of a large passenger jet with 257 people aboard that flew from New Zealand to Antarctica in 1979. Unbeknownst to the pilots, the flight coordinates had been modified just two degrees, meaning that the plane was twenty-eight miles east of where the pilots assumed it to be. This resulted in the airplane flying into the side of a twelve thousand-foot volcano, killing everyone on board. Elder Uchtdorf concluded,

> Through years of serving the Lord and in countless interviews, I have learned that the difference between happiness and misery in individuals, in marriages, and families often comes down to an error of only a few degrees. . . . These commandments and covenants of God are like navigational instructions from celestial heights and will lead us safely to our eternal destination. It is one of beauty and glory beyond understanding. It is worth the effort. It is worth making decisive corrections now and then staying on course.[6]

Commandments and covenants are the needles on the ball that keep us on a straight course. And thus we see that "by small means the Lord can bring about great things" (1 Nephi 16:29). Every one of us can access our own personal Liahona. And we don't even have to wait in line!

Family Feud: What to Do When the Kids Want to Kill Each Other (1 Nephi 17–19)

In most scriptural stories (as with any form of literature), there is usually a point of no return where the conflicting actions of the characters slowly compound to create a combustible situation that finally explodes. The narrative of Nephi and his brothers is reminiscent of the biblical experience of Joseph and his brothers, as the angry siblings head toward the breaking point. One tense scene occurred on the ship when the rebellious Laman and Lemuel and some of the sons of Ishmael started to party with their wives. Nephi rebuked them for their lightheartedness, and they got so angry they decided it was time to silence that annoying voice of his once and for all.

> And after we had been driven forth before the wind for the space of many days, behold, my brethren and the sons of Ishmael and also their wives began to make themselves merry, insomuch that they began to dance, and to sing, and to speak with much rudeness, yea, even that they did forget by what power they had been brought thither; yea, they were lifted up unto exceeding rudeness.
>
> And I, Nephi, began to fear exceedingly lest the Lord should be angry with us, and smite us because of our iniquity, that we should be swallowed up in the depths of the sea; wherefore, I, Nephi, began to speak to them with much soberness; but behold they were angry with me, saying: We will not that our younger brother shall be a ruler over us.
>
> And it came to pass that Laman and Lemuel did take me and bind me with cords, and they did treat me with much harshness; nevertheless, the Lord did suffer it that he might show forth his power, unto the fulfilling of his word which he had spoken concerning the wicked. (1 Nephi 18:9–11)

Family Violence

It may seem farfetched to imagine your own children involved in a struggle so violent that somebody gets bound with cords and requires an angel's intervention, but violence in families is extremely common. If you've never experienced it, then you are fortunate—probably in the minority of the earth's population. Every nine seconds in the United States, a woman is assaulted or beaten; around the world, one in three women has suffered abuse during her lifetime.[7] Brothers fight, sisters fight, parents hit their children and each other, and sometimes children abuse their parents. Even among families that are not physically violent, emotional and mental abuse may occur on some level at great cost to those who suffer it.

Anyone who has raised a family knows what I'm talking about. By the time I had four small children, I'd learned that my father's fiery temper (of which I was so critical as a child) had definitely been passed along to me. I'd go along just fine, displaying all of the qualities of patience and tolerance good mothers have, and then suddenly I'd just lose it. (I once heard my own temperament described as "nice, nice, nice, nice . . . boom!")

Thankfully, a good upbringing taught me to bridle that passion so I didn't lose control, abuse my children, or kick the dog. But feeling that emotional upheaval was really humbling and made me recognize the fine line between anger and abuse. Anyone, under the wrong conditions, can go over that line.

It Can Happen to Anyone

In a wonderful little book titled *Thoughts of a Grasshopper*, Louise Plummer courageously talked about a difficult son who struggled with anger issues. Week by week, year by year, he sabotaged family meals, devotionals, and gatherings with cruel remarks and increasingly violent behavior until he reached the breaking point:

> One sunny afternoon in Saint Paul, Minnesota, that same boy lunged at me, grasped me around the throat in a headlock, pulled me to the floor and said, strangling me, "Don't tell me what to do, or I'll kill you. Do you hear me? I'll kill you." And he tightened his grip. I believed he would kill me. I relaxed my whole body, went limp, and let him threaten me until his energies wore out. Then I said, "Let go of me now." And, finally, he did.[8]

Louise went on to describe her hurt, humiliation, and anger at the unfairness of her situation. After all, she had been good all of her life, said her prayers, kept the commandments, and tried to do everything God asked of her. Why should she be in such a situation? "I raged metaphorical fists at God," she said. "Why me? And the answer was always the same: 'Why not you?' Sometimes living in a family means suffering. The truth, I know now, is that a peaceful, loving, Mormon family is an ideal."[9]

You Are Not Alone

If you've experienced violence—or any form of physical, emotional, or mental abuse in your family—the book of 1 Nephi lets you know you are not alone. Though they were children of loving parents, Laman and Lemuel became angry enough to want to kill their brother Nephi and actually attempted to do so a couple of times. Is there anything we can learn from this deeply divided family?

To begin with, there is a lot of comparing going on here. I can't help placing myself in the sandals of Lemuel and Laman, wondering how I would have felt as Lehi admonished them often to be more like their younger brother. This never went over well, and it clearly worked against Nephi by making them angrier.

But on the other hand, what was Lehi to do? He clearly realized his two oldest sons were unbelievers, and he was panicked about their futures. Nephi wrote, "They knew not the dealings of that God who had created them" (1 Nephi 2:12). Back in Jerusalem, their indifference to spiritual things probably hadn't mattered all that much, but when Lehi's religious devotion was causing the family to suffer poverty and dislocation, their lack of faith no doubt was painfully obvious, and dissensions came to the surface.

In our own families these conflicts may arise over a temple wedding from which some family members are excluded or the insistence of one spouse on paying tithing or observing the Sabbath while the other has different priorities. These divisions can be difficult and painful for every member involved.

The sad truth is that when we have family members who are divided in their beliefs, we will have family members who are divided in their behavior. Some will be conservatively dressed on Sunday and attend church, while others may be headed to the movies or to a champagne brunch. This can make it fairly difficult to dwell in harmony, especially when one family member feels called upon to correct the others. I think it is significant here that what the brothers resented most was not that Nephi refused to join the party, but that he preached at them: "We will not that our younger brother shall be a ruler over us" (1 Nephi 18:10.)

Not All the Time, Just Betimes

Perhaps a lesson we can learn from Lehi's fractious family is that we need to carefully choose our battles. Especially when our children are grown, it creates real problems if we are continually correcting them or if they are continually correcting each other. Though others' behaviors may sadden us, corrections should be few and far between or else the relationship will gradually deteriorate. The Doctrine and Covenants offers a valuable bit of counsel on just how much we should try to correct others: "Reproving betimes with sharpness, *when moved upon by the Holy Ghost*; and then showing forth afterwards an increase of love toward him whom thou hast reproved, lest he esteem thee to be his enemy; that he may know that thy faithfulness is stronger than the cords of death" (D&C 121:43–44; emphasis added).

The word *betimes* can be defined two ways: speedily or occasionally. If we apply both meanings, we may infer that when the Holy Ghost inspires us to reprove someone, we should do so *immediately*. However, this should only happen *occasionally*, and then even more love should be shown thereafter, "lest he esteem thee to be his enemy" (D&C 121:43). It's clear that, though Nephi's intentions were undoubtedly pure, Laman and Lemuel saw him as an enemy. Given the situation, this might have been unavoidable, but Nephi's frequent reproofs probably didn't help. On the other hand, if Nephi's brothers were creating an intolerable environment for him and his family, something had to be said. We often face similar conundrums in our individual lives and homes.

The crucial point here is the motivation; we trust that Nephi was moved upon by the Holy Ghost before he spoke up, and we should be too. The spouse who, after days, weeks, or even years of love and acceptance, speaks up in the power of the Spirit and lets her husband know that he is on a wrong course is on a much stronger footing than the wife who nags her husband every day. He knows "that [her] faithfulness [to him] is stronger than the cords of death" (D&C 121:44). She is not an enemy; she is his truest and most faithful friend. And if she waits for the Holy Ghost to choose the moment and give the words, he might just listen.

Deposits and Withdrawals

Steven Covey famously used the metaphor of an emotional bank account that exists between two people. If we continually deposit love, acceptance, and positive affirmation, we can occasionally make a withdrawal when it is really needed by offering some constructive criticism or even a stern rebuke.[10] Even then, as the scripture teaches, we must follow that withdrawal with additional deposits, specifically "an increase of love" (D&C 121:43).

I had a revealing conversation that illustrated this point with a friend of mine who is gay. Reared in a devoutly Catholic home, he is now married to an LDS man, and they are raising an adopted daughter together. He told me how, in an effort to stay close to their respective families, they traveled (rather nervously) to Idaho to attend a reunion of the LDS partner's extended family. This was, of course, a difficult situation for everyone involved and represents a challenge that many of us face in our own families today. As this couple made their way into the family home, a cousin and her husband came up, greeted them, and then said, "We just want you to know, we love you but hate what you're doing."

My friend said, "I know that this cousin was just trying to be sure we understood their position on gay marriage, but believe me, *we understand their position*. It would've meant so much to us to simply be greeted with love."

This well-meaning cousin did not have a relationship of love and trust with this couple, and without that they "esteem[ed her] to be [their] enemy" when she offered corrections. As a result, they were hurt rather than helped by her comments, however well intended. When in doubt about whether to correct someone, I try to visualize the image of Jesus, silently writing in the sand while the elders of the church condemned the woman taken in adultery. If He, the great Judge of all mankind, was slow to condemn, how much more should we, who are full of sin, wait for the prompting of the Holy Ghost before we presume to correct another.

Let the Holy Spirit Guide

With this in mind, Nephi's words in 1 Nephi 17:45 take on added importance, as he explained to his brothers why they were unable to discern divine direction: "Ye are swift to do iniquity but slow to remember the Lord your God. Ye have seen an angel, and he spake unto you; yea, ye have heard his voice from time to time; and he hath spoken unto you in a still small voice, but ye were past *feeling*, that ye could not *feel* his words; wherefore, he has spoken unto you like unto the voice of thunder, which did cause the earth to shake as if it were to divide asunder" (emphasis added).

What is necessary to "feel" the guidance of the Holy Ghost? For one thing, it appears that quiet is required, for He speaks in a "still small voice." As Catherine Thomas said, "Divine voices are speaking all around us, but our hearing doesn't hear and our seeing doesn't see. Until finally it does."[11] Sensitivity to the whisperings of the Holy Ghost is apparently a learned skill, and without that divine inspiration we may be doing more damage than good in our dealings with loved ones.

Division in families may inevitably occur as a result of religious differences, but we sometimes make it worse than it needs to be and possibly make it harder for the Savior to reach those we love. I believe that we'll be accountable to Christ for the judging, divisive comments we make that were not inspired by the Holy Ghost, but rather were said out of fear, narrow-mindedness, or lack of faith in the power of Christ. On the other hand, if we consciously construct relationships on eternal love in those moments when the Holy Ghost moves upon us, we may confidently speak up with power and say what needs to be said, no matter how unpleasant or socially awkward. If this happens rarely (betimes), it will have an impact that is far different than the constant harping we sometimes fall into.

A Lehi Moment

I witnessed an example of this the year that my husband's father turned ninety, and the family gathered to celebrate. As the luncheon drew to a close, it would've been easy just to disperse, but my courageous father-in-law chose instead to bear his testimony. Several of his children and grandchildren are estranged from the Church, and there were also several in the room who are not members. I'd say that at least half of the people there were made quite uncomfortable by this good man's remarks as he solemnly bore his witness of the Prophet Joseph Smith, the Book of Mormon, and the saving power of Jesus Christ.

Don Faulkner is one of the kindest and most accepting men I know; he is not a "preachy" guy and generally goes out of his way to make everyone feel welcome. So when he stood up and began to bear his testimony, I was deeply touched by his courage and faith. He was clearly moved upon by the Holy Ghost, and his testimony will stand; his posterity will be answerable for whether or not they took heed. It was a moment worthy of Lehi.

Notes

1. Richard Neitzel Holzapfel, Dana M. Pike, and David Rolph Seely, *Jehovah and the World of the Old Testament* (Salt Lake City: Deseret Book, 2009), 208.

2. Marcus J. Borg and John Dominic Crossan, *The First Christmas: What the Gospels Really Teach About Jesus's Birth* (New York, HarperCollins, 2007), 25–35.

3. John Welch, "Chiasmus in the Book of Mormon," *New Era*, February 1972.

4. See a diagram of the chiasmus found in Alma 36 in *Book of Mormon Student Manual, Religion 121–122* (Salt Lake City: The Church of Jesus Christ of Latter-day Saints, 2009), 232.

5. John Welch, "Chiasmus in the Book of Mormon," *BYU Studies* 10:1.

6. Dieter F. Uchtdorf, "A Matter of a Few Degrees," *Ensign*, April 2008.

7. See http://www.ncadv.org/learn/statistics.

8. Louise Plummer, *Thoughts of a Grasshopper: Essays and Oddities* (Salt Lake City: Deseret Book, 1992), 82.

9. Ibid., 45–46.

10. Stephen R. Covey, *The 7 Habits of Highly Effective People: Powerful Lessons in Personal Change* (New York: RosettaBooks, 2013), 197–98.

11. M. Catherine Thomas, *The God Seed: Probing the Mystery of Spiritual Development* (Salt Lake City: Digital Legend Press, 2014), 106.

Your Stories and Thoughts

_____

_____

_____

_____

_____

_____

_____

_____

_____

_____

_____

2 Nephi: Out of One Wilderness and into Another

The Parable of the Promised Land (2 Nephi 1)

In Lehi's final message to his sons and daughters, he assured them that the Lord had prepared a land of promise for His faithful children. "But, said he, notwithstanding our afflictions, we have obtained a land of promise, a land which is choice above all other lands; a land which the Lord God hath covenanted with me should be a land for the inher-itance of my seed" (2 Nephi 1:5).

At this point in the narrative, Lehi's family had been wandering in the wilderness for years, literally and figuratively. While Nephi and his followers had chosen to find God there, Laman and his followers had chosen to become even more spiritually lost than they'd been in Jerusalem, going so far as to plot the death of their own brother. Now, as he approached his own demise, Lehi's description of their future prospects can be taken literally and figuratively.

Lehi said that if his disobedient sons thereafter chose to "reject the Holy One of Israel . . . he will bring other nations unto them, and he will give unto them power, and he will take away from them the lands of their possessions, and he will cause them to be scattered and smitten" (2 Nephi 1:10–11). In contrast, he described Nephi and his obedient children thus: "And if it so be that they shall serve him according to the commandments which he hath given, it shall be a land of liberty unto them; wherefore, they shall never be brought down into captivity. . . . And if it so be that they shall keep his commandments they shall be blessed upon the face of this land, and there shall be none to molest them, nor to take away the land of their inheritance; and they shall dwell safely forever" (2 Nephi 1:7, 9).

We'll see that the promised land, as a metaphor for spiritual well-being, is a central theme throughout the narrative.

How Do We Inherit the Promised Land?

What is the promised land for us, and how do we come to inhabit it? The obvious interpretation of the promised land is as a reference to the Americas and its inhabitants, but, like the prophecies of the Old Testament, there may be more than one layer of interpretation available. Lehi's comments about the promised land and his own spiritual condition in comparison to that of his sons gives us a sense of what the promised land might symbolize.

The promised land, according to Lehi, is a land of liberty and safety. To lose the blessing of the promised land is to be brought into captivity by "other nations," or foreign powers (2 Nephi 1:11). So what is our own spiritual "promised land?" The obvious answer would be the celestial kingdom—our eventual reward for righteous living, where surely there will be peace and safety (and none of those scary foreign powers). But Lehi isn't just talking about a future reward or a physical promised land. He said, "But behold, the Lord hath redeemed my soul from hell; I have beheld his glory, and I am encircled about eternally in the arms of his love" (2 Nephi 1:15). In other words, though he still lived in a world of strife and travail, Lehi was already inhabiting the spiritual promised land.

Following Christ isn't just a case of enduring sorrow on earth to gain a reward in heaven, nor is it a condition of unease about our eventual reward. According to Lehi, we don't have to go through life wondering if we'll be exalted. As we accept Christ as our Savior, we then enter into a state of grace and live, "encircled about eternally in the arms of his love" (2 Nephi 1:15). The spiritual promised land isn't just a reward in heaven; it's also happening right here. It comes with the change of heart that brings a quiet assurance that we are Christ's spiritual children and He will bring us home.

Lehi connects the two concepts—the promised land and a lively hope in Christ—with this beautiful concluding image: "And he hath said that: Inasmuch as ye shall keep my commandments ye shall prosper in the land; but inasmuch as ye will not keep my commandments ye shall be cut off from my presence" (2 Nephi 1:20). The presence of Christ in our lives is the promised land.

This theme—the rebirth of the spirit that causes us to dwell in a "land of promise" (2 Nephi 1:3), even as we are surrounded by the wilderness of the world—lifts the prophecy from a focus on a particular geographical location to one that applies to every human soul. As followers of Christ, we're living in the promised land right now. And you know what they say about real estate: location, location, location!

Four Prophetic Perspectives

The book of 2 Nephi features four separate voices: Lehi, Nephi, Jacob, and Isaiah, each with its own tone and emphasis. Mormon had all of the records at his hands and made decisions about what to leave in the final record that would be buried away for a future prophet to find. It is significant that he chooses to include all four of these prophetic voices.

Faced with limited space, Nephi chose to devote much of his record to the prophecies of Isaiah, and Mormon (faced with even more limited space on one set of plates for a thousand years of history) elected to keep them. Both prophets were compiling their records toward the end of their lives, and Isaiah's prophecies apparently struck a chord with them.

The book of 2 Nephi is light on action and heavy on prophecy. After the death of Lehi, the two groups (led respectively by Nephi and Laman) separated and abandoned any hope of reconciliation. The Nephites built a temple and kept the law of Moses, in preparation for the coming of the Savior, who was first seen in Nephi's vision, and then further attested by Jacob's visions and his interpretation of the visions of Isaiah.

Agency: Are We Really Free to Choose? (2 Nephi 2)

Lehi asserted that the Fall was necessary so that mankind would have agency, which is the definition of freedom. "And because that they are redeemed from the fall they have become free forever, knowing good from evil; to act for themselves and not to be acted upon. . . . Wherefore, men are free according to the flesh . . . and they are free to choose liberty and eternal life, through the great Mediator of all men, or to choose captivity and death" (2 Nephi 2:26–27).

Philosopher David Hume defined liberty as "a power of acting or of not acting, according to the determination of the will."[1] Lehi said essentially the same thing but went one step further, asserting that we're "free to choose liberty and eternal life" or "captivity and death" (2 Nephi 2:27). This suggests that using our freedom to make right choices leads to ever-expanding ranges of choices that open up as we go forward. Conversely, wrong choices have a restricting power on our liberty—freedom to make choices diminishes as we choose poorly—until we are made captive by consequences and eventually are destroyed spiritually.

These days, there is some debate about how autonomous people really are. Do we really have the ability to make choices, or are our lives determined by nurture, nature, and hosts of other causes? The Book of Mormon takes a firm stand on this issue: Men and women are "free according to the flesh; and all things are given them which are expedient unto man" (2 Nephi 2:27). According to Lehi, our futures are not predetermined; we can choose and will be accountable for our choices. Of course, there are mitigating factors. (Philosophers sometimes speak of "free willings," referring to the intention of the mind and heart, even if circumstances beyond control prevent action according to will.) But even with that caveat, the Book of Mormon is "pro-choice" in the most literal sense. We can determine our destinies and indeed must do so; it's the purpose of our existence.

Teaching Our Children to Choose for Themselves

How does the question of agency affect our roles as parents? One of the greatest challenges parents face is deciding how much freedom to allow their children at a given time, as well as how much to shield them from the consequences of wrong choices. In fact, the baby boom generation has given rise to a new term: a helicopter parent. Defined as "a parent who pays extremely close attention to a child's or children's experiences and problems, particularly at educational institutions," a helicopter parent is so named because he or she hover over his or her children.[2]

As parents, we have high expectations for our children, and we often fear that allowing them to fail at anything will adversely affect their lives. Research shows, however, that taking choices away from children to protect them may actually impede development of crucial brain functions such as problem solving and impulse control. "[Teenagers] are developing experiences, learning from the experiences and creating synaptic pathways," said Frances Jensen, author of *The Teenage Brain: A Neuroscientist's Survival Guide to Raising Adolescents and Young Adults.* "It's a learning time. You have to learn from experience. . . . Parents should make sure they stay out of the day-to-day trial and error, because your kid is going to need to use that experience to learn when to take a risk and when not to take a risk."[3]

Are We Helping or Hurting Our Children?

When our oldest son went to college, there were two boys living in the dorm whom no one saw often. It wasn't until the end of the first semester that their families realized these two young men never actually went to class! Finding themselves unsupervised (probably for the first time in their lives), they proceeded to play video games all day, every day until they were both expelled. This is an extreme example, but it does raise the question of how much damage we do when we hover over our kids. Most of us have rescued a child when he or she left a project or paper until the last minute, and many of us feel that we earned several of the merit badges on that Scout uniform or deserve that grade on the AP exam. Are we doing our children a favor when we continually rescue them, or are we actually crippling them in some way?

Larry Nelson, a professor of family life at Brigham Young University, said we may be doing just that: "Overall, stepping in and doing for a child what the child developmentally should be doing for him or herself, is negative. . . . Regardless of the form of control, it's harmful at this time period."[4] It's sobering to realize that we may actually be impeding the development of our children's brains by shielding them from the full decision-making process, including the consequences of their mistakes.

One family we admire has a policy of *not* reminding their children about papers, quizzes, upcoming projects, and so on. Once their children leave elementary school, they are expected to keep track of their own assignments without the usual nagging from the parents. Nobody gets rescued at the last minute, and as a result nearly all of them have embarrassing failures along the way. The parents find, however, that after one or two of these crises, the lessons are learned—and by the time they get to high school (where the grades really count), their children have learned to take responsibility for their own school performance.

Better Choices Make Us Freer to Choose

An interesting facet of agency is that certain choices inhibit our ability to make more choices and other choices enhance that ability. An obvious example is the choice to use addictive substances. Once we become addicted, the freedom to choose is greatly inhibited. Less obvious, but equally constricting, may be the choices we make that create fears and phobias.

In the book *Sway: The Irresistible Pull of Irrational Behavior*, Ori and Rom Brafman identified a variety of attitudes that govern our decisions, from loss aversion to the chameleon effect. There are countless ways the human mind is influenced in making choices: "We're constantly sending and receiving cues and subtle messages to and from one another—swaying and being swayed, even if our rational brain hasn't been let in on the secret."[5] Only through the Spirit can we see clearly (see 1 Corinthians 13:12). Simply being aware that our minds are subject to influence from myriad sources helps us understand why freeing ourselves from selfish and carnal motives increases our ability to truly act for ourselves.

Are the Scriptures Literature?

You might feel an instinctive negative reaction to looking at the scriptures as literature because literature is often fictional. But the word *literature* refers to the way things are said rather than whether the material is factual or fictional. It's been said that history is an account of what happened, while literature is an account of what happens. In other words, literature attempts to recreate human experience in such a way that a personal and even a universal application may result. This is a perfect description of what the scriptures do so beautifully. They are factual and true, and they are also literature in the highest sense of the word.

The Book of Mormon, according to scholar Grant Hardy, includes a wide variety of literary devices: "The Book of Mormon draws on the same set of narrative tools used by both novelists and historians, including direct and indirect speech, digressions, framing narratives, quoted documents, metaphors, allusions, juxtapositions, explicit commentary, variations in duration, chronological disruptions, repetitions, contrasts, motifs, and themes."[6]

Nephi Psings a Psalm (2 Nephi 4)

Psalms, as a literary form, were an important part of Hebrew worship and would have been well known to Nephi. It was a form also used by several other religious cultures living in the region, including the Egyptians and the Syro-Palestinians.[7] Along with being expressions of praise, lament, or faith, psalms also had a definite liturgical purpose as part of temple worship. Because one of Nephi's first priorities in the new world was to build a temple "like unto Solomon's temple" (2 Nephi 5:16), this is significant. John Gabel stated, "The prevalent theory now is that most (if not all) of the poems in the psalmbook were used in ceremonies at the Second Temple—sung or chanted with musical accompaniment at various points in the ritual."[8]

The Psalms feature a formal "envelope" structure that usually opens with a theme that is repeated at the end. The internal structure of the Psalm may feature several types of parallelism. Here's how it works: The Psalm opens with a statement, adds a variation of that statement, and perhaps even another variation after that. Then it retreats back to the second point, and then back to the first.

Parallelism: Say It Again, Sam

Here's a short explanation of the three kinds of parallelism you will find in the Psalms:

- Synonymous—saying the same thing twice: "Wherefore, when I came, there was no man; when I called, yea, there was none to answer" (2 Nephi 7:2).
- Antithetic—contrasting two opposite ideas: "For the heavens shall vanish away like smoke, and the earth shall wax old like a garment; and they that dwell therein shall die in like manner. But my salvation shall be forever, and my righteousness shall not be abolished" (2 Nephi 8:6).
- Progressive—expanding on an image or idea: "Therefore, the redeemed of the Lord shall return, and come with singing unto Zion; and everlasting joy and holiness shall be upon their heads; and they shall obtain gladness and joy; sorrow and mourning shall flee away" (2 Nephi 8:11).

Nephi used all three kinds of parallelism in his psalm, which is written in the deeply formal style he would have learned as a Jewish boy. A great deal of composition goes into a psalm like this; though it feels like an emotional outpouring, it is actually a controlled expression, created within an established framework. Here is just a small snippet from Nephi's "lament." If you look closely, you can find all three types of parallelism here:

> Nevertheless, notwithstanding the great goodness of the Lord,
> in showing me his great and marvelous works,
> my heart exclaimeth: O wretched man that I am! [Antithetical.]
> Yea, my heart sorroweth because of my flesh;
> my soul grieveth because of mine iniquities. [Synonymous.]
> I am encompassed about, because of the temptations and the sins which
> do so easily beset me.
> And when I desire to rejoice, my heart groaneth because of my sins;
> [Progressive]
> nevertheless, I know in whom I have trusted. (2 Nephi 4:17–19)

Why Use Poetry in the Scriptures?

At this point, you might be asking yourself what the purpose of a psalm is. Why go to all the trouble of expressing something in such a formal, repetitive manner, rather than just saying it in plain language? The answer lies in the way that poetry affects our brains. There is something powerful in poetic form that might be compared to compressing molecules into a small space; it unleashes power. The careful construction that goes into a poetic expression increases its impact.

Let me illustrate: Each year, I go to England for a couple of weeks of literary study, and I consider it a fun challenge to try to pack for the whole trip in one carry-on bag. To do this, each article of clothing has to perform several functions—a dress or a jacket must be versatile enough to be worn a few different ways, and everything in the bag must be color coordinated. The same is true of the elements in a good poem. Each word and image should have several layers of meaning, calling to mind other poetic expressions as well that will increase the depth of the reading experience. The poem has a greater impact than simple prose, because each word has been chosen deliberately to offer several layers of meaning.

Write Your Own Psalm

If you've ever whiled away the time on a road trip with a *Mad Libs* book, you know it can be fun to use random parts of speech to create silly poems. Let's try doing something similar with the Psalms, just to get the idea of how they are made. Then, for a more serious version, we'll fill in the blanks to create a psalm of praise.

My House Is Psuch a Mess

My house is a _____ (noun—simile)

It is like a _____ (noun—simile)

My neighbor's house is a _____ (use a visual image—a metaphor)

But my house is a _____ (use the opposite image)

My kids' rooms are _____ and _____ (adjectives)

Their clothes are like _____ (noun—simile)

And their toys are _____ (noun—simile)

I want a new house that _____ (describing phrase)

And new kids who _____ (describing phrase that builds on it)

Then I would be truly _____ (adjective)

And my home would be a _____ (noun—metaphor)

I'm Getting Psomewhat Old

I am _____ (describe your condition)

My body is like a _____ (noun—simile)

I used to be a _____ (use a visual image—a metaphor)

But now I am _____ (use the opposite image)

Every day, I _____ (verbs that describe your difficulties)

In the morning _____ (add more detail)

At night _____ (add more detail)

I miss the days of youth, when _____ (describe activity or condition)

And I was like a _____ (noun—simile)

But those days are gone, like _____ (describe how they disappeared)

And I am _____ (restate first line a new way)

A Pserious Psalm of Praise

The Lord is _____ (describe your perception of Him)

He _____ (restate it differently)

Other people are _____ (metaphor)

But the Lord is a _____ (metaphor)

When I need help _____ (describe how He helps you)

And He _____ (more detail)

And He_____ (more detail)

I want to _____ (describe a desire you have
about God)

And long to _____ (restate differently)

Because He _____ (restate your perception of Him)

And I know he will _____ (restate differently)

Did Joseph Smith Simply Copy the Isaiah Chapters?

One of the most common criticisms leveled against Joseph Smith is that he just took large portions of the King James Bible and put them in the Book of Mormon. Joseph Smith undoubtedly used the Bible as a reference when he came upon these passages, but he made over four hundred changes to them. Scholars have tried to find reasons for his variant readings (such as changing those verses where italics occur), but his changes don't appear to follow any set pattern.

In a few places, Joseph made changes that would have been imposs-ible for him to know about if he didn't have a unique text in front of him. One in particular occurs in 2 Nephi 12:16, which reads, "And upon all the ships of the sea, and upon all the ships of Tarshish, and upon all pleasant pictures." The King James Version that Joseph would have referred to reads, "And upon all the ships of Tarshish, and upon all pleasant pictures" (Isaiah 2:16). The Septuagint version (a version Joseph almost certainly never saw) reads, "And upon all the ships of the sea, and upon all pleasant pictures." The fact that Joseph Smith's version incorporates both seems to indicate that he was translating from a document that predated both the Septuagint and the King James Version.[9]

The Isaiah Passages: Why We'd Better Not Skip This Part (2 Nephi 12–24)

If it feels like we get a really big helping of Isaiah in the Book of Mormon, it's because we do. Scholar Monte S. Nyman provided the following stats:

> There are sixty-six chapters, containing a total of 1,292 verses [which includes ninety verses not written by Isaiah—Chaps. 36–39] in the present-day KJV text of Isaiah. Nineteen of the sixty-six chapters are quoted in their entirety in the Book of Mormon, and two other chapters are quoted in their entirety except for two verses in each chapter. The first two verses of one other chapter are quoted in the Book of Mormon, and one verse from each of two other chapters. Eight chapters of Isaiah have verses quoted from them more than once, either completely or partially. Not counting these duplications, 425 of the 1,292 verses of Isaiah are quoted in the Book of Mormon. Of these 425 verses, 229 are quoted differently from those in the King James text, while 196 are identical.[10]

There is no way around the fact that the Isaiah passages are long and difficult to understand. So why should we make the effort to read Isaiah? Here are three reasons:

Because it's hard. At times, we might be tempted to believe that Nephi was just messing with our minds when he claimed to love the words of Isaiah. The language of Isaiah is stylized and symbolic, and his cultural and historical references can be rather confusing. In other words, he makes us work! Nephi does admit that Isaiah is hard for most of us: "For behold, Isaiah spake many things which were hard for many of my people to understand; for they know not concerning the manner of prophesying among the Jews" (2 Nephi 25:1). Perhaps Nephi wanted us to know not just what Isaiah has to say but where he is coming from. Describing his people as "a branch that has been broken off" from the house of Israel, he said, "Hear ye the words of the prophet, which were written unto all the house of Israel, and liken them unto yourselves, that ye may have hope as well as your brethren from whom ye have been broken off" (1 Nephi 19:24). This mental work is great preparation for the rest of the Book of Mormon.

All the best people are reading him. In addition to Nephi, Jesus Himself said that Isaiah was well worth our effort. "Behold, I say unto you, that ye ought to search these things. Yea, a commandment I give unto you that ye search these things diligently; for great are the words of Isaiah. For surely he spake as touching all things concerning my people which are of the house of Israel; therefore it must needs be that he must speak also to the Gentiles. And all things that he spake have been and shall be, even according to the words which he spake" (3 Nephi 23:1–3). Hugh Nibley (with his characteristic snarkiness) quipped, "The book of Isaiah is a tract for our own times; our very aversion to it testifies to its relevance."[11]

Isaiah has a worldview we need right now. Isaiah brings a perspective that is surprisingly savvy; he often sounds as if he is describing our day. Hugh Nibley pointed out that the sins Isaiah condemned and the virtues he praised may surprise us. He zeroed in on the dangers of avarice, greed, status-seeking, and obsession with physical appearance. In contrast, "In Isaiah's book, the qualities that God demands of men are such as our society looks down on with mildly patronizing contempt. Isaiah promises the greatest blessings and glory to the meek, the lowly, the poor, the oppressed, the afflicted, and the needy."[12]

So, though you may be tempted just to skip him, Isaiah is worth the wrestle—not in spite of his difficult language, but rather because of it. Remember, poetic language packs a punch that prose doesn't; each word is carefully chosen to convey layers of meaning. The poetry is supposed to strike you and get your attention.

Nephi concluded, "The words of Isaiah are not plain unto you, nevertheless they are plain unto all those that are filled with the spirit of prophecy" (2 Nephi 25:4). This tends to intimidate me until I remember that "the testimony of Jesus is the spirit of prophecy" (Revelation 19:10). As long as we keep Jesus squarely in the middle of what we are reading, we can't go too wrong in Isaiah.

Nephi, Isaiah, and Joseph

There is another interesting aspect to the Isaiah passages: the triangle of authors involved. Nephi, using the brass plates of Laban, began by choosing the passages of Isaiah that he felt would be of most benefit to his people and was then offering commentary on many of them, applying them to his own history. Then Joseph Smith translated Nephi's redaction of Isaiah. Grant Hardy saw the multilayered and complex personality of Nephi emerging in these chapters:

> Not only does Nephi shape his narratives with particular ends in mind but he also interprets scripture in intricate ways. We have seen long quotations followed not by detailed commentaries but by fresh prophecies that expand on particular themes. . . . Nephi deliberately rereads the Bible with his own situation in mind, and he finds himself in Isaiah's ancient prophecies. . . . Clearly there is an active mind at work here, one that is colored by his experiences, his sense of audience and his desire for order.[13]

Isaiah Goes to Girls' Camp (2 Nephi 27)

In Judaism, the Midrash is a method of interpreting biblical stories that goes beyond a simple distillation of religious, legal, or moral teachings. It fills in gaps left in the Bible's narrative and attempts to solve the problems in interpreting difficult passages in the Torah or the five books of Moses.[14]

The use of the Midrash would've been a familiar practice to Nephi and Jacob, and they both offered examples of it in this record. In 2 Nephi 6–10, Jacob quoted from the book of Isaiah and compared the passages to the events that were transpiring in the Nephite nation. Though Jacob was reading Isaiah's words about the exile of the Jerusalem Jews to Babylon, he saw a direct connection to his own group and their self-imposed exile to the New World. As members of the house of Israel, Jacob said, they were free to interpret these verses in relation to their own experiences.

Jacob showed us with his Midrash how to take the words of Isaiah and apply them to our own lives. So let's take a passage and engage in a little Midrash madness of our own.

Inviting Isaiah to Camp

I've spent many of my years in the Church serving in the Young Women organization—fifteen of those years putting on girl's camp. (I personally feel that this should assure my exaltation.) Camp traditionally ends with a testimony meeting, where the girls have a chance to get up and express how they've been affected by their camp experience. These are, of course, tearful, emotional meetings. (With two hundred girls involved and forty to fifty exhausted leaders, there are bound to be lots of tears!) But over the years as I planned our camp activities, I began to worry that what we were creating there was perhaps not as substantive as it should be. The girls would get all worked up, but within a few days all that good camp mojo seemed to drain away, and life went back to its old patterns. Were we really changing lives? I wasn't quite sure what to do about it.

Then one day, I was struggling through the Isaiah passages in the Book of Mormon and came upon this little gem: "And all the nations that fight against Zion, and that distress her, shall be as a dream of a night vision; yea, it shall be unto them, even as unto a hungry man which dreameth, and behold he eateth but he awaketh and his soul is empty; or like unto a thirsty man which dreameth, and behold he drinketh but he awaketh and behold he is faint, and his soul hath appetite; yea, even so shall the multitude of all the nations be that fight against Mount Zion" (2 Nephi 27:3).

At first glance, this wouldn't seem to apply to a bunch of teenaged girls; they aren't nations fighting against Zion (though random acts of violence may occasionally occur in cabins filled with pubescent girls). But the image of the hungry dreamer struck me and made me think about how emotion can be a deceptive substitute for real change. We may get worked up and feel ready to reform our lives, but after the excitement of the meeting, we are like the hungry man who dreamed about a yummy dinner but woke up just as empty as before. Isaiah's words showed me why these girls were coming to camp and getting emotionally wrought up, but a lasting change of heart was not occurring in their lives. They were being emotionally stimulated rather than spiritually filled.

So what was the answer? Nephi said that the key to Isaiah is the spirit of prophecy, or the testimony of Jesus. So I began to think about what we were doing specifically to build the testimony of Jesus in the girls' hearts. From then on, year by year, we tried to emphasize gaining a knowledge of the Savior and His Atonement in our lessons, devotionals, messages, and private discussions with girls. We began to make a conscious effort to bring Christ into the camp experience.

Converting Campers to Christ

Once we shared our new vision with them in our training meetings, our wonderful camp counselors really poured their hearts into centering their lessons on Christ. Each day they taught a devotional centered on some aspect of the Savior's Atonement. On the final day, each group found a quiet spot, and a special lesson was given on the parable of the ten virgins. As this hour drew to its close, our stake president (dressed in his Sunday best) walked around to each group and quietly invited them all to come with him because the "bridegroom was come." The girls, surprised by his sudden appearance in their midst, went reverently, spontaneously singing hymns along the way, and gathered in the amphitheater, where a large picture of the Savior was displayed. Our sweet stake president bore a powerful testimony of the Savior and invited them to do the same.

The difference in that meeting was palpable. Certainly there was emotion, but the testimonies (which in former years had focused mostly on friends and family) were centered on the Lord and His redeeming love, which they had felt all week. That love poured out on our gathering like a little Pentecost. I felt afterward that the testimonies borne that day were substantive; they were still there the next morning and in subsequent weeks and months. This experience taught me that Jesus is truly the Bread of Life. Anything else is just spiritual snack food, an illusion that leaves you hungry later. I have Isaiah to thank for that lesson.

So gird up your linguistic loins and make your way through Isaiah—maybe with a goal to find just three or four things about which you can make little Midrash lessons that will apply to you and your calling or your kids or job. If you give Isaiah a chance, I think you'll find that there is some really good stuff there.

How Much Do We Really Talk about Christ? (2 Nephi 25)

"And we talk of Christ, we rejoice in Christ, we preach of Christ, we prophesy of Christ, and we write according to our prophecies, that our children may know to what source they may look for a remission of their sins" (2 Nephi 25:26).

As Latter-day Saints, we have so many facets to our faith that it's easy to miss the source of living water in a discussion of the various tributaries. But when it comes right down to it, we either talk about Christ, rejoice in Christ, and preach of Christ or we don't. People who know us well either regard us as devout Christians or they don't, based on our behaviors in those three areas.

A young woman named Vivian Harmer discovered this while she was studying at a university in northern England. One day, she rode on a bus with an Evangelical Christian who, when she learned that Vivian was Mormon, flatly stated, "Mormons aren't Christians." Of course Vivian denied this and asserted that we really are Christians. Her seatmate replied that she'd once been visited by the Mormon missionaries, who claimed they had a message for her about Jesus Christ. "I let them in to talk about Christ," she said, "and all we talked about was some man named Joseph Smith. I don't believe in him, and they didn't tell me about Christ. Your church isn't Christian."[15]

For the first time, Vivian realized that there may be a reason why Latter-day Saints are often considered to be something other than devout Christians. Nephi's words from this passage came to mind, and she began to examine her own patterns of conversation, especially in regard to her missionary efforts. To her surprise, she realized that she could recall many gospel conversations where she had covered a variety of topics—from the Book of Mormon to living prophets to the pioneers—but had somehow failed to mention that the point of all of it was to lead us to Christ, whom we worship and adore, and by whose grace we are saved.

In describing his daily walk with Christ, Nephi also gently challenges us to take a close look at ours. Do your children, grandchildren, and friends hear you talk about Christ, rejoice in Christ, and preach of Christ? Do they see you looking to Him (rather than to programs or goal-setting sessions) for a remission of your sins? Are you a person who speaks often and freely about grace? In other words, are you easily identifiable as a born-again, saved-by-grace Christian, as well as a commandment- and covenant-keeping Mormon? After all, the whole point of the covenants and the commandments is to lead us to the rebirth of the Spirit and the outpouring of grace that only comes from the Savior. In his second book, Nephi taught that our faith in Christ should be so obvious to our neighbors that they should laugh if anyone describes us as anything other than followers of Jesus.

How Do Mormons Praise the Lord? (2 Nephi 33)

"I glory in plainness; I glory in truth; I glory in my Jesus, for he hath redeemed my soul from hell" (2 Nephi 33:6).

As Latter-day Saints, we can be a little awkward about praising the Lord, can't we? Our Evangelical Christian neighbors raise their hands and shout out an amen, but we are rather shy about such emotional outbursts. I like to compare Mormon culture to an old married couple who really do love each other but don't feel the need to say it out loud. However, Nephi had no hesitation about expressing praise (in fact, he sounds a little like an old-fashioned Pentecostal preacher), and I think he has something to teach us. How should we offer praise to the Lord? Here are three ways we might take the praise up a notch without going too far out of our comfort zones:

Sing the hymns—don't mumble. Our hymns are our psalms. They exist to help us express, through poetic language and rhythmic music, our deep feelings of reverence for God. Why then don't we sing out? Nothing brings the Spirit more quickly than singing, but it's rare to see a congregation really sing with enthusiasm. As a lesser talent in a family of singers, I was often shy about raising my voice, and my brother Marty (a marvelous vocal coach) would say to me, "Just make your sound, Marilyn." The same goes for you—just make your sound, whatever it is. When the hymn starts, sit up and raise your voice in song.

Praise the Lord in your prayers. Remember how Jesus taught us to pray? The Lord's Prayer begins and ends with a "praise phrase": "Hallowed be thy name" and "For thine is the kingdom, and the power, and the glory, for ever" (Matthew 6:9, 13). Jesus instructed us, "After this manner therefore pray ye" (3 Nephi 13:9), so perhaps we ought to begin and end our prayers with words of praise.

Praise the Lord in your conversation. I co-taught seminary with a wonderful woman named Brenda Smart, who began each lesson by asking the students to share how they were guided by the Spirit that week. We all got into the habit of giving credit where credit was due: to God. Do your children or grandchildren hear you talk about daily miracles and how the Lord has blessed you in small ways? We can acknowledge the Lord's hand in our lives more consistently and courageously. That is part of standing as a witness.

Notes

1. David Hume (1748, section viii, part 1), as quoted in "Free Will," *Stanford Encyclopedia of Philosophy*, http://plato.stanford.edu /entries/freewill.

2. See en.wikipedia.org/wiki/Helicopter parent.

3. Caroline Gregoire, "Extra Love Doesn't Make Up for Negative Effects of Helicopter Parenting, Study Finds," *Huffington Post*, posted June 2015.

4. Larry Nelson, as quoted in Brooke Adams, "Extra love and support doesn't make up for being a helicopter parent," *BYU News Release*, http://news.byu.edu/print.aspx?id=22452.

5. Ori and Rom Brafman, *Sway: The Irresistible Pull of Irrational Behavior* (New York: Crown Business, 2008), 109.

6. Grant Hardy, *Understanding the Book of Mormon: A Reader's Guide* (New York: Oxford University Press, 2010), 9.

7. Robert Alter, "Psalms," *The Literary Guide to the Bible* (Cambridge, Massachusetts: Harvard University Press, 1996), 244.

8. John B. Gabel, Charles B. Wheeler, and Anthony D. York, *The Bible as Literature: An Introduction*, third edition (New York, Oxford University Press, 1996), 19.

9. Terryl Givens, *By the Hand of Mormon* (New York: Oxford University Press, 2002), 137.

10. Monte S. Nyman, "Restoring 'Plain and Precious Parts': The Role of Latter-day Scriptures in Helping Us Understand the Bible," *Liahona*, December 1981.

11. Hugh Nibley, "Great Are the Words of Isaiah" *Sperry Symposium Classics: The Old Testament*, edited Paul Y. Hoskisson (Provo and

Salt Lake City: Religious Studies Center, Brigham Young University, and Deseret Book, 2005), 177–95.

12. Ibid.

13. Grant Hardy. *Understanding the Book of Mormon*, 83–84.

14. *Paperback Oxford English Dictionary*, seventh edition (Oxford: Oxford University Press, 2012).

15. Vivian Harmer, "We Talk of Christ," *New Era*, April 1987.

Your Stories and Thoughts

_____

_____

_____

_____

_____

_____

_____

_____

_____

_____

Jacob: A Temple, a Tree, and a Traitor

Healing Wounds: What Really Goes on in the Temple (Jacob 1–4)

Temples arouse a lot of curiosity among our neighbors from other faiths. Because we restrict entry to worthy recommend holders and are known to worship differently in the temple than in regular church services, many wonder what we are really up to in there. Well, we're up to something wonderful in the temple, though it's not nearly as sensational as our neighbors might think. What we are actually doing is learning about our place in the great scheme of things and making promises to God through covenants.

The book of Jacob gives a good idea of how the temple figures into our faith. As the book opens, it has been fifty-five years since Lehi's family left Jerusalem. At this time, Nephi was an old man and had passed the kingship on to a successor (unnamed for us because succeeding kings were simply called second Nephi, third Nephi, and so on). Jacob and Joseph, Nephi's younger brothers, had been "consecrated priests and teachers of this people, by the hand of Nephi" (Jacob 1:18). Jacob then received a direct revelation from God that inspired the opening discourse of his record: "As I inquired of the Lord, thus came the word unto me, saying: Jacob, get thou up into the temple on the morrow, and declare the word which I shall give thee unto this people" (Jacob 2:11).

According to Jacob, the Nephites were guilty of three sins: "[They] began to grow hard in their hearts, and indulge themselves somewhat in wicked practices, such as like unto David of old desiring many wives and concubines, and also Solomon, his son. Yea, and they also began to search much gold and silver, and began to be lifted up somewhat in pride" (Jacob 1:15–16). Though they had been an obedient people, Jacob saw a gradual decline into class distinctions based upon wealth and status, distinctions that were causing some to suffer at the hands of others. The people, in other words, were losing their perspective about possessions, forgetting that all that they had came from God.

So Jacob went into the temple and preached a sermon that covered three topics that are still paramount themes in every temple worship service: charity, chastity, and consecration.

Charity, Chastity, and Consecration

Elder James E. Talmage described the temple endowment in this manner:

> The ordinances of the endowment embody certain obligations on the part of the individual, such as covenant and promise to observe the law of strict virtue and chastity, to be charitable, benevolent, tolerant and pure; to devote both talent and material means to the spread of truth and the uplifting of the race; to maintain devotion to the cause of truth; and to seek in every way to contribute to the great preparation that the earth may be made ready to receive her King—the Lord Jesus Christ. With the taking of each covenant and the assuming of each obligation a promised blessing is pronounced, contingent upon the faithful observance of the conditions.[1]

In the temple, we promise to be a certain kind of person, and we promise it solemnly, in the presence of God and angels. No wonder President Boyd K. Packer cited the covenants made in the temple as the source of the Church's power.[2] Covenants in relation to the three principles of charity, chastity and consecration are at the center of the endowment service.

Charity: Avoiding the Deceitfulness of Riches

The book of 2 Nephi features four narrative voices, all of which have something to say about materialism and pride. Jacob built on Isaiah's comments about the love of money and the pride that often accompanies having more than our neighbors, going right to the cause of class warfare, discrimination, and most of the social ills that beset us: "Because some of you have obtained more abundantly than that of your brethren ye are lifted up in the pride of your hearts . . . and persecute your brethren because ye suppose that ye are better than they" (Jacob 2:13).

Even though we know that money doesn't buy happiness, our actions often proclaim the opposite idea put forward by the adversary, which is that you can buy anything with money. Most of us spend inordinate amounts of time thinking about, talking about, spending, earning, and wasting money on "that which is of no worth . . . [and] cannot satisfy" (2 Nephi 9:51). This obsession with material things is a central theme in Isaiah, and Jacob brings it right into our daily lives with his challenge to "think of your brethren like unto yourselves, and be familiar with all and free with your substance, that they may be rich like unto you. But before ye seek for riches, seek ye for the kingdom of God" (Jacob 2:17–18).

Chastity: Healing the Deep Wounds

Jacob's tone then grew surprisingly tender as he moved from the issue of pride to moral purity. He worried about being forced to use "much boldness of speech concerning you, before your wives and your children, many of whose feelings are exceedingly tender and chaste and delicate before God, which thing is pleasing unto God" (Jacob 2:7).

Jacob saw sexual infidelity as the potential destroyer of the Nephite people, and we can apply his warnings to a new threat that causes so much heartbreak today—pornography. His words describe its destructive potential with eerie foresight: "Ye have broken the hearts of your tender wives, and lost the confidence of your children, because of your bad examples before them; and the sobbings of their hearts ascend up to God against you. And because of the strictness of the word of God, which cometh down against you, many hearts died, pierced with deep wounds" (Jacob 2:35).

In the introduction to Gary Wilson's groundbreaking book *Your Brain on Porn*, Professor Andrew Jack summed up the problem of pornography:

> Technology is in danger of making us impersonal, of dampening our capacity and tendency for human connection. Perhaps the most important example of the way that digital technology allows us to withdraw from ordinary interaction is pornography. In a healthy relationship, sex is associated with the highest levels of intimacy and trust. It is, or at least can be, the culmination and expression of our closest human connection. It not only helps to reinforce this connection, it also creates entirely new life. . . . [This drive] has been essential to the flourishing of the human race. Yet pornography transforms that drive into a force that primarily motivates the completely solitary and unproductive activity of masturbation.[3]

Wilson described experiences with hundreds of young men who found themselves no longer able to function normally in intimate relationships. Not only had they "lost the confidence" of wives and children, but they had also actually lost the ability to function as men; "many hearts died, pierced with deep wounds" perfectly describes the pain suffered by those lured into the illusion of "harmless" pleasure that porn offers (Jacob 2:35).

Fighting Fire with Fire

What does Jacob offer as a solution to this type of evil? Then and now, his solution is dramatically simple and direct: He urges us to throw ourselves upon the mercy of Christ, the only being who wields power great enough to overcome the terrifying influence of the adversary. Jacob shows us exactly how to draw upon the power of the Atonement and promises power to overcome evil through grace: "Wherefore, we search the prophets, and we have many revelations and the spirit of prophecy; and having all these witnesses we obtain a hope, and our faith becometh unshaken, insomuch that we truly can command in the name of Jesus and the very trees obey us, or the mountains, or the waves of the sea. Nevertheless, the Lord God showeth us our weakness that we may know that it is by his grace, and his great condescensions unto the children of men, that we have power to do these things" (Jacob 4:6–7).

So if you or someone you love is struggling with addiction of any kind, Jacob's words are a key to overcoming its destructive power. When we immerse ourselves in the word, we receive revelation in our hearts, and the spirit of prophecy (meaning the testimony of Jesus) gives us hope. With that hope, our faith can become unshakeable enough to defeat our adversary—whether it be pornography, drugs, alcohol, or any other pernicious threat. Jesus Christ is great enough to conquer the soul-crushing threat of pornography, a cancer that is literally destroying a generation of people and causing untold misery for those with whom they have lost the power to be truly and purely intimate.

Virtue and chastity may be out of fashion, but that doesn't make them old-fashioned. Instead, they are timeless principles of power. Recently, a friend who is a Christian pastor asked me about our temple worship service. I mentioned to him that there are five covenants we make every time we go and gave him the overview I quoted previously from Elder James E. Talmage. "Wait a minute," he said with a chuckle. "By 'strict virtue and chastity,' are you saying that every time you go to the temple, you actually promise not to have sex with anyone but your spouse?"

I replied, "Well, you're a minister. Do you think it would be a good idea for all of your married parishioners, say on a monthly basis, to raise their right hands and swear to be faithful to their spouses?"

The scoffing chuckle died as he gave that some serious thought. Quietly, he replied, "It would be the best thing in the world."

The firm decision to be virtuous and chaste is one of the keys to happiness in marriage and peace in life. It is a decision we formally restate each time we go to the temple.

Consecration: Knowest Thou the Condescension of God?

From chastity, Jacob went on to talk about repentance in general. In doing so, he echoes Nephi's teaching on the condescension of God, or how low God would go to rescue us. And the means of that rescue are always miraculous. Jacob indicates that as we come to understand the depth of God's love (notice the word *depth*: love condescends; it goes deep down), it unleashes a power within us so great that we can command in the name of Jesus and be obeyed. The steps to tapping into this powerful love are listed: read the word, seek revelation and a testimony of Jesus, obtain a hope in Him, and then grow in faith until it becomes unshakeable and command the miracle in the name of Jesus Christ, knowing that the power comes only through His grace.

Notice what Jacob does *not* say. He doesn't suggest a long to-do list of behavioral changes. He doesn't say that you have to be worthy before the miracle happens, or that you must be doing everything right to merit the Atonement. No, the merit belongs to Jesus; we just have to believe and have faith. The miracle is there to help us become worthy; we don't have to overcome our sins and weaknesses before turning to God. Just search the prophets, said Jacob, and they will point you to Jesus, the source of the power.

The process of repentance requires us to draw upon the saving power of Christ's grace, and consecration is its natural outgrowth. As we receive the love of God and taste of the fruit, our hearts become knit to His. When it comes to His devotion to us, Christ is all in. Are we?

The temple is a step-by-step tutorial in consecration, in giving our lives to God. We begin with the covenant to obey, and then we promise to make sacrifices when needed and to make changes in our behavior to be worthy of His Spirit. We promise complete fidelity to those who are bound to us by covenant. Finally, with these promises as a foundation, we are ready to make the ultimate vow: to completely consecrate ourselves to Christ and His kingdom. As a result, we are promised blessings that are beyond imagining, and we leave feeling a measure of that power blessing our everyday lives. Tapping into the power of Christ's love through our promises—that's what really goes on in the temple.

Career Planning for Women with the Allegory of the Olive Tree (Jacob 5)

Erma Bombeck said: "We've got a generation now who were born with semi-equality. They don't know how it was before, so they think, this isn't too bad. I come from a generation of women who went to bed because their husbands were tired."[4] In her inimitable way, Erma summed up the mindset that spawned the women's movement—fighting the idea that women's needs, desires, and contributions were somehow less important than those of men. This push for equal rights with men has been a central focus of progressive women for hundreds of years, and the battle is by no means over. Though women represent a large faction of the workplace, the White House reported that full-time working women earn, on average, just seventy-seven cents for every dollar a man earns.[5] Yet equal rights means more than being paid the same as men or having the right to vote. It means feeling that a woman's choices (whether they be about bedtime or career paths) are as viable and valuable as a man's. That continues to represent a seismic cultural shift worldwide.

Be Careful What You Wish For

Generations of women have worked and sacrificed so that women today have the freedom to choose to do whatever they want with their lives; for many of us, that day is here. Freedom is an exhilarating, terrifying thing, isn't it? "What do I want to do?" It's not a simple question. For a woman, the decision to focus on a demanding career may affect whether she marries, whom she marries, how many children she bears, and how they are reared. On the other hand, the decision to stay home and rear a family of children may prevent her from pursuing a rewarding career or contributing in other ways to the world at large. These are important concerns; they involve decisions that are eternal in nature. As LDS women, we want to live lives of service yet not be relegated to the status of a martyr. We want to use our gifts for good yet we don't want to be deceived in our priorities. How do we find the right path?

As a young mother, I faced these same concerns. While I longed to continue my education and have opportunities to expand my gifts, I also wanted to raise a large family of children and be home with them; I wanted to do it all! I had mixed feelings. On the one hand, I thought it unfair that women with strong desires to continue in their careers while raising families be censured for that choice. On the other hand, I felt defensive when women treated me as somehow inferior because I chose to be at home with my little ones. In an attempt to make sense of the issue, I wrote these words:

> I am one among a generation of highly educated women who have been exposed to the excitement of the marketplace, stage, office, or studio. We have achieved and have struggled to make a place for ourselves. We have been leaders, missionaries, and executives. We have traveled and written and been written about. And for most of us, marriage and the birth of that first child have brought us face to face with a difficult question: "Must I give all of this up in order to raise a family?" Somehow, I feel socially and intellectually frustrated in the traditional role, but spiritually and emotionally frustrated outside of it. Oddly enough, I find myself ashamed to admit to being just a homemaker and ashamed to admit to being otherwise!

Zenos Comes to the Rescue

During this time, I found an answer (of all places) in the allegory of the olive tree. The parable tells of an ailing orchard that is treated by the lord of the vineyard and his servants. They begin by grafting some wild branches into natural trees that bear fruit, but the fruit all turns out tainted. At this point, the lord, in frustration, suggests that they wipe out the whole crop and wonders, "Who is it that has corrupted my vineyard?" (Jacob 5:47). His servant replies with this astonishing bit of wisdom: "Is it not the loftiness of thy vineyard— have not the branches thereof overcome the roots which are good? . . . Behold they grew faster than the strength of the roots, taking strength unto themselves" (Jacob 5:48).

So the lord and his servants begin grafting natural branches back into the tree while pruning back the wild branches, taking special care to keep "the root and the top thereof equal, according to the strength thereof" (Jacob 5:73). Soon, everything is back to rights; the fruit is good—that which "was most precious unto him from the beginning" (Jacob 5:74). The lord and his servants rejoice, and the allegorical house of Israel thrives.

The Olive Tree and Me

Though I'm sure the prophet Zenos wasn't thinking of working moms when he chiseled this onto the brass plates, here is how this allegory seemed to apply to me as a young mother. I saw my branches as the talents and accomplishments that the world sees and my roots as my character and spiritual strength. It was easy to see how quickly my branches could overgrow my roots were I just to concentrate on my ambitions and accomplishments. Motherhood and the sacrifice of being with my young children caused me to step back for a time from more visible pursuits, in effect pruning off some branches. It was painful; it felt like sacrifice. But I could see that this pruning could be spiritually valuable, and I wanted to be where I was most needed. So I embraced that time with faith that God had my back. In retrospect, I can see how those years of quiet service to my family allowed me to send my roots down deep into the soil and become a different person than I would've been without them. The years out of the limelight were a gift, not a burden.

But it's seldom just one thing or the other. At the same time we were having our children, I was helping my husband start a family business that involved creating marketing materials for financial professionals. We've done this together over the last thirty years and have built two businesses, which have provided for our family and offered employment to many others. Craig was always mindful of the need to put our children first, and for the most part I was able to help with the business while staying at home with our kids, but not always. There were times we both felt stretched to the breaking point.

Susan Tanner, former general Young Women president, shared a personal story about needing to be two places at once, something all women understand. She felt a great need to be at the side of a daughter who had a difficult and risky pregnancy, but she was scheduled to go on a world tour for the Young Women. She prayed in faith and received the blessing she needed, walking off the plane just in time to be there for the birth.

I think a key point here is the nature of the miracle she asked for; she asked for help, not for the problem to go away. Like most women, I must make daily, sometimes hourly, decisions about where to be and whom to serve. Reminding myself that there are always going to be "root days" and "branch days" has helped me navigate the daily dilemmas about whether to be home with little ones, over at the office, fulfilling a Church calling, writing a book, or taking a needed day off! When I get overwhelmed, I try to remember that "only God can make a tree" and ask Him to help me prioritize.

Pick Up Your Shovel and Get to Work

Another important lesson from the allegory of the olive tree relates to how we see ourselves as workers in our own little house of Israel—our family. I'm often quite surprised when I see women who have free time every day—because their children are either in school or out of the home—but who feel no need to contribute when the family is struggling financially. The husband may be overwhelmed with financial challenges, and yet the wife may feel that it is not her place to help. In the allegory, the servants don't stand around arguing who should prune and who should shovel; everybody just gets to work!

The role of the man as the main provider does not mean, in my opinion, that a woman need not help, any more than a woman's role as the main nurturer excuses the man from doing everything he can in that area as well. "The Family: A Proclamation to the World" states, "In these sacred responsibilities, fathers and mothers are obligated to help one another as equal partners."[6] Isolating ourselves within preconceived roles is not only limiting, it may even work against the ultimate objective we seek.

Can We Have It All?

As I left college, my mentor, Arthur Henry King, handed me the "BYU Honors Reading List" and challenged me to read everything on it. I fell short of completing that lofty goal, but I did make a real effort to read as many of the books on that list as I could over the next fifteen years as I raised our five children. The day our last child started preschool, I drove straight down to the state university and started my master's degree on a part-time basis.

I will never forget that first day; it was already two weeks into the semester, and I nervously found a seat in a room full of people half my age. The kind professor made me feel welcome, opened the book, and began to read Wordsworth. Nothing has ever sounded sweeter. After fifteen years of studying on my own, I was so thrilled to be in a classroom again, reading poetry with people who chose to be there, that I shed tears of joy. I appreciated that moment so much because I had paid a real price for it. I'd used my "root" years to prepare, and now I was there—not for the degree, nor for the praise of others, but because those years had taught me who I was and what I really loved to do. I was ready to branch out and bear some fruit.

Over the next five years, I enjoyed the experience of expanding my mind (and doing homework right along with our children) and eventually earned that degree, which in turn led to a variety of opportunities that have enriched my life (and I hope others' lives too). It's been a confusing, winding road; it's also been a deeply satisfying one. I have no regrets, nor do I feel like I have given up one thing to do another. With the help of the lord of the vineyard, I've felt guided each step of the way, and I "have joy in the fruit" (Jacob 5:71).

Plan for a Long, Productive Life

So what wisdom does the allegory offer the women of today? For several years, I served the young women in the Church, both in a ward and in a stake. Whenever I was asked to speak, I encouraged girls to be realistic in their educational choices and to aim high—not just for a job, but for a career that would enable them to do whatever is needed to achieve the divine injunction to raise righteous families. So many girls choose to pursue some version of "education-lite," believing that they will never be called upon to contribute to the family income, though statistics reveal this to be wishful thinking in most cases. When reality strikes and they find that they must make a contribution, many are disappointed to find that they must work many hours away from home because their training was inadequate. Perhaps with better planning, those crucial years of education could have been used to train for a profession that would have allowed them to work half as many hours for twice as much pay.

For example, if you love books, add an editorial component (proofreading, technical writing, and so on) to that English major. The Internet is loaded with content that needs to be written by someone; copywriters and editors make good money, and many of them work from home! If you're good at numbers, aim high and become a CPA. My daughter-in-law, Megan, is a great example of smart choices in education. She earned an accounting degree and worked for one of the large firms until she married our son. That preparation allowed her to take a position as CFO for a small company, and they have worked with her to allow her to work from home as children came. As our son's career and their family have grown, she has reduced her workload. All of this was possible because she prepared herself through wise educational choices.

Another young woman I know, who had a goal to become a pediatrician, began to retreat from that goal when she married. She thought perhaps she should just become a physical therapist. Her father gave her some great advice in two words: "Aim high." She prayerfully chose to train as a physician's assistant and graduated just as her first child arrived. With that training, she is prepared to assist in supporting the family if needed and will go on to earn a maximum return for the minimum hours away from home. In addition, she accomplished a goal that was important to her and stands as an equal partner to her husband.

What You Do Matters, Eternally

The allegory of the olive tree teaches that every tree in the vineyard is precious to the lord, and he desires that each one achieve its full potential. The message I take from that is to nourish both root and branch. Prepare for a career that allows you to make a contribution in the world while also spending the maximum amount of time at home with your children. This, in my view, is very much in the spirit of "The Family: A Proclamation to the World." When we combine this message with the parable of the talents, which teaches us to develop our gifts as fully as possible, we have a practical guideline for life. It makes good sense to become all that you can, knowing that, in the Lord's time, your contribution will be called for.

And this allegory isn't just for young women; I've seen so many women in their fifties and sixties who have ample time for productive second careers but feel a bit lost because they have never planned ways to use their gifts after those two or three decades when children were in the home. After the busy years of mothering, it becomes hard to simply kill time, and depression can easily set in when a woman feels less needed. Again, I quote my thirty-year-old musings:

> How then shall I, as a Mormon woman, succeed in nourishing both root and branch equally? There is no easy answer to this dilemma, and I'm content with the confusion that many options bring. The allegory of the olive tree has helped me sort out my own experiences, past and present, and see the importance of the less glamorous times. I have realized that my frustration at having to lay aside certain areas of endeavor for others is not the abandoning of my potential, but merely the temporary pinch of pruning. I have realized in retrospect that many accomplishments in my life were born out of a selfish desire for applause; these wild branches with tainted fruit sap the strength from the weak roots. I have seen in clearer perspective the value of the long, difficult growing times when there is no spotlight, no ego gratification—only the duty to be done, along with a constant sense of my inability to do it alone.
>
> All women have these times if their lives are in balance, but perhaps we do not appreciate the value of those growing periods. In the wisdom of the lord of the vineyard, the days of blossoming will come again, and then the fruit that is produced will be sweeter and closer to that natural fruit that the lord loves, with all of the wild, impure elements removed.

Lose Your Life to Find It

Author C. S. Lewis wrote, "The essence of religion in my view is the thirst for an end higher than natural ends: the finite self's desire for and acquiescence in, and self-rejection in favor of, an object wholly good and wholly good for it. That the self-rejection will turn out also to be a self-finding, that the bread cast upon the waters will be found after many days, that to die is to live—these are the sacred paradoxes."[7]

Looking back now, thirty years after writing about this allegory, I feel grateful for the guidance it gave me. Rather than selfishly pursuing my passions, I've tried to bring passion to whatever I've been given to do, knowing that doing so would help my roots go down deep and allow the branches to blossom in God's time. I haven't made much progress, but I know I'm on the right road. I knew it then too, but reading my words from those days reminds me that those first steps were shaky: "After our hard-fought battle for freedom to choose, the trusting of one's destiny to anyone, even a loving Father, is a frightening proposition. Yet it appears that true balance, true fulfillment, and true growth can only be found through total submission to the lord of the vineyard. To me, this is the greatest step in life, and I'm not sure I have accomplished it; I feel instead that I am in midair. Yet, in the light of our current cultural challenges, perhaps we need that balancing hand more than ever before."

Today, just as I did then, I lose my balance at times. When I do, I go back to the allegory of the olive tree and remember what that pinching and pruning and grafting is all about: "That the root and the top may be equal in strength, until the good shall overcome the bad . . . and the good will I preserve unto myself" (Jacob 5:66, 77).

Notes

1. James E. Talmage, *The House of the Lord* (Salt Lake City: Deseret Book, 1976), 84.

2. *Preparing to Enter the Holy Temple* (Salt Lake City: Intellectual Reserve, 2002), 36.

3. Gary Wilson, *Your Brain on Porn: Internet Pornography and the Emerging Science of Addiction* (Kent: Commonwealth Publishing, 2014).

4. Erma Bombeck, as quoted in Carolyn Warner, *Treasury of Women's Quotations* (New York: Pearson, 1997).

5.   See https://www.whitehouse.gov/equal-pay/career.

6.   "The Family: A Proclamation to the World," *Ensign*, November 1995, 102.

7.   C. S. Lewis, *A Mind Awake: An Anthology of C. S. Lewis*, edited by Clyde S. Kilby (Boston: Mariner Books, 1968), 111.

Your Stories and Thoughts

Enos, Jarom, and Omni: Big Ideas in Small Packages

The Wrestling Match: Getting Answers to Prayer (Enos)

"I will tell you of the wrestle which I had before God, before I received a remission of my sins" (Enos 1:2). Wrestling has been called the world's oldest form of competition and was widely practiced long before its appearance at the first recorded Olympic games in Greece in 776 BC.[1] The word *wrestle* comes from the Old English word *wrest*, meaning to "pull, detach, [or] take by force."[2]

It's interesting that in at least two places in the scriptures, wrestling is used as a metaphor for prayer. The account of Jacob wrestling with the angel of the Lord to obtain a blessing was recorded on the brass plates and would undoubtedly have been part of what Enos described as the teachings of his father (see Enos 1:1). Thus, it isn't surprising that he used the wrestling metaphor when describing his long struggle in prayer.

Through Prayer, Enos Is Born Again

One commentary explained Jacob's wrestle with the angel as a search for a new identity: "In antiquity, it was believed that selfhood was expressed in the name given a person. Jacob's new name signified a new self: no longer was he the supplanter, but Israel, which means 'God rules.'"[3] The wrestle in prayer is like a labor and delivery, and Jacob, the trickster who liked to win at any cost, was reborn as Israel, father of nations.

Because Enos went through a similar struggle, he emerged with a new view of himself and his role in the lives of others. In his book, he said that the impetus for his supplication to God was a longing to feel the "joy of the saints" (Enos 1:3). He obviously knew the gospel teachings, but somehow the joy had eluded him. Enos prayed all day and into the night, and then finally heard a voice that assured him his sins were forgiven. In amazement, he asked, "Lord, how is it done?" and received the startling information that a Being whom he hadn't ever seen had been the means of forgiving his sins (Enos 1:7–8). Enos had heard of Christ, but he now had a direct experience with the Savior, and it changed him.

After his sins were forgiven, Enos immediately thought about his brethren and prayed for them. After securing a promise that they would be visited by the Lord's grace, Enos's heart expanded even more, and he began to pray for his enemies (though he also called them his brethren), the Lamanites. He had a specific request—that the Lord would preserve the sacred records and make sure that the Lamanites got them at some point. God granted this request and mentioned that Enos's fathers had asked the same thing (Enos 1:9–18).

Under the influence of the Savior's grace, Enos moved quickly in an outward direction, from praying for himself to praying for his loved ones to even praying for his enemies.

Your Wrestling Match with God

Do you ever feel like you are in a bit of a wrestling match with the Lord? We all have certain things we want—for ourselves and for our loved ones—and yet it may seem like we pound on the doors of heaven but some things never change. What can we learn from Enos about getting answers to prayers? Here are three things his experience has taught me:

Real prayer is hard work. When God invites us to pray, He takes is seriously. He stated, "Ask, and it shall be given you" (Luke 11:9).

Obviously His definition of the word *ask* is a little different than the casual endless requests that often constitute our prayers. Just think about the number of things we ask God for every day! (And some of them are kind of crazy, like praying that a favorite sports team will win or that God will cause a molecular change to occur in the red punch and sugar cookies so that they will miraculously be "nourishing and strengthening to our bodies.") We may need to rethink the meaning of the word *ask* in our lives. How much effort are we putting into our prayers?

In a religion class, we were challenged to pray aloud for fifteen minutes every day. That doesn't seem difficult until you try it. Most of us found that we were out of things to say after five minutes, but Enos prayed all day and all night. That takes some spiritual muscle. Perhaps one of the reasons God required Enos to pray for all that time before he got what he asked for was so he would take it as seriously as God does and so he would be strong enough to handle the answer when it came.

"How" is a better question than "why." We spend a lot of time in life asking "why me?" or "why now?" or "why this trial?" and so on. I've never had much luck with such questions (though I've asked in tears with fists clenched), and I have found it more useful to set those questions aside and ask one that works better. Enos's question, "Lord, how is it done?" leads to insights about the Atonement and Christ's endless love. The question of why we must endure certain trials may be too much information for us right now. I imagine the Lord just smiling when I ask those "why" questions and filing an answer away in my heart that will emerge when I'm ready.

By the way, there is one prayer I can pull out like a favorite fishing lure, to which I can always get an answer: "Lord, give me something to do." I'm really not yet capable of understanding why most things happen to me. I'm always capable of doing some act of service, however, and because He has a long list of errands that need running, I have pretty consistent luck with just asking for a task. Enos followed that pattern, and he got everything he asked for.

The purpose of prayer is *not* to get the things you want. We pray about stuff all the time: worries, fears, and temporal things we need. But the purpose of prayer is not to get (or not get) what we want from God. The purpose of prayer is to change our hearts. Enos knelt down and prayed because "his soul hungered" (Enos 1:4). That hunger was satisfied, and he felt the "joy of the saints" he had heard about (Enos 1:3).

Enos went into his prayer with a hungry soul and came away a new man, which is evident in the way his life changed. As a prince of the realm, he would certainly have been in line to be king, and he seemed to have had plenty of time to go hunting and think about himself. But after this prayer, Enos spent the rest of his life preaching to anyone who would listen, "testifying of the things which I had heard and seen" (Enos 1:19). After that experience, he would certainly have agreed with Gandhi, who said, "Prayer is not asking. It is a longing of the soul. It is daily admission of one's weakness. It is better in prayer to have a heart without words than words without a heart."[4]

Enos's final words show how completely his prayer was answered. The joy that he expressed in anticipation of a reunion with his beloved Savior sends chills down my spine. This privileged but uncertain young man had indeed become a savior on Mount Zion, with his calling and election made sure. "And I soon go to the place of my rest, which is with my Redeemer; for I know that in him I shall rest. And I rejoice in the day when my mortal shall put on immortality, and shall stand before him; then shall I see his face with pleasure, and he will say unto me: Come unto me, ye blessed, there is a place prepared for you in the mansions of my Father" (Enos 1:27).

The Power of Prayer

Alfred Tennyson reminded us that prayer has real power to it and behind it:

> Pray for my soul. More things are wrought by prayer
> Than this world dreams of. Wherefore, let thy voice
> Rise like a fountain for me night and day.
> For what are men better than sheep or goats
> That nourish a blind life within the brain,
> If, knowing God, they lift not hands of prayer
> Both for themselves and those who call them friend?
> For so the whole round earth is every way
> Bound by gold chains about the feet of God.[5]

The Word's Worth: The Purpose of the Scriptures (Jarom and Omni)

The book of 1 Nephi really contains two distinct narratives. The first (chapters 1–9) is an abridgement of Lehi's records. The second (chapters 10–22) is Nephi's story, as recorded on the second set of plates he made.

In both narratives, Nephi combined personal experiences with passages from the brass plates (the Torah) to illustrate the principles he wanted to teach. He even quoted whole chapters from Isaiah. (By the way, if you feel weary reading these chapters, just think of the effort required to transcribe such long passages onto metal plates!)

Nephi showed some concern about the things he was choosing to include and the things he was leaving out, but he let us know that these choices were governed by one overriding purpose: "And I, Nephi, have written these things unto my people, that perhaps I might persuade them that they would remember the Lord their Redeemer" (1 Nephi 19:18).

As the record was passed from Nephi to his brother Jacob, who then passed it to his son Enos, we begin to see how a deep commitment to keep these records was ingrained in the hearts of the Nephite leaders. Even those who were not faithful to the commandments (like Omni) were faithful in keeping and passing along the sacred record.

Notes

1. "History of Wrestling," see http://wrestling.isport.com/wrestling -guides/history-of-wrestling.

2. "Wrest," *Online Etymology Dictionary*, http://etymonline.com /index.php?allowed_in_frame=0&search=wrest&searchmode =none.

3. *The New Oxford Annotated Bible: New Revised Standard Version* (New York: Oxford University Press, 1991), 43.

4. Mahatma Gandhi, *Goodreads*, http://www.goodreads.com/quotes /41191-prayer-is-not-asking-it-is-a-longing-of-the.

5. Alfred Tennyson, "Morte D'Arthur," *Poems* (London, Moxon, 1845).

Your Stories and Thoughts

Words of Mormon: A Brief Word from Our Sponsor

The Things of My Soul: Mormon and Scrapbooking

A redactor sounds like a creature out of *Jurassic Park*, but the word means something less than an author but something more than an editor. A redactor takes a batch of texts and turns them into one cohesive book. So we might imagine Mormon sitting in a room with the brass plates of Laban, the large and small plates of Nephi, and the records of the Jaredites and the other various "-ites" who populated the New World and faced with the challenge of turning all of them into one record. How did he do it?

Mormon shares with us his criteria for choosing among the multiplicity of records available to him: "And the things which are upon these plates pleasing me, because of the prophecies of the coming of Christ; and my fathers knowing that many of them have been fulfilled . . . and as many as go beyond this day must surely come to pass—wherefore, I chose these things, to finish my record upon them . . . and I cannot write the hundredth part of the things of my people" (Words of Mormon 1:4–5).

When I was a young wife and mother, it was the age of scrapbooking. I was never good at it, but occasionally I would attend a workshop or

101

see a friend doing it, and I'd get all excited about documenting our family life in scrapbooks. I would go spend a few hundred dollars on archival paper, cute stickers, fabulous leather binders, and special pens. Then I would come home and begin making elaborate pages about family events. This state of excitement would last for a few weeks until something else would get my attention. Eventually the project would stall, and my husband would shake his head and try not to say, "I told you so."

I'm nearly forty years into my marriage now, with lots of kids and grandkids. Those pathetic attempts at scrapbooking are still hidden away in a cupboard that looks like what Mormon's record room must have looked, except with stickers. It's a mess. But somehow, Mormon managed to make sense of those piles of records and create something that has lasted through the generations—he reminds me that I have the same responsibility as the chief record keeper for our family.

Every one of us must decide (not just on a daily but often on an hourly basis) how to prioritize the information that comes to us. We cannot take it all in or pass it all on. We must choose what to retain and what to discard. What can we learn from Mormon about controlling and curating information?

Let's take a look again at Mormon's criteria for choosing what items to include in his record: He chose things that were pleasing to him and spiritual in nature, and he edited down the materials so that they were easily accessible to the generations that would follow. Let's think about how we might follow his pattern.

Choose Things That Are Pleasing to You

Mormon noted that other records had exhaustive accounts of the wars and contentions of the people, but he chose to transcribe the records that were more spiritual in nature. Nephi said of them, "Upon these [plates] I write the things of my soul" (2 Nephi 4:15).

Make a record of the things of your soul. I don't think this means you should just bear your testimony every time you write in your journal. The things of your soul might include music you love, poetry, books, media, scriptures, or thoughts. Or things like talks that touch you, conversations you have, prayers you see answered, or miracles in your life. Things of your soul might include times of discouragement, doubt and worry, or repentance and forgiveness. (The things of my soul are often questions I struggle even to articulate, let alone answer.)

We don't need to keep every program and playbill, but it's really great if those who come after us have some record of what thrilled our souls.

Choose Things That Are Spiritual in Nature

In college, my branch president challenged me to write my thoughts in a notebook as I read the four Gospels. At the end of that exercise, I had a little notebook about Jesus and me, and I had a hope in Christ that changed my life. I wish I had that notebook now; it is something I wish I could have passed on to my children and their children. Mormon chose what to put in and what to leave out, so he chose things that focused on Christ.

This year, I've invited my Book of Mormon class to make a "Jesus Book" as they read. Everything they learned about Christ in the Book of Mormon should go in there. They are creating a precious treasure for those who come after them.

To have a little book that recorded the ways you walked with the Savior on a day-to-day basis would be a pearl of great price for anyone who loves you. And it would be something you could go back and read when your faith falters. As Alma said, "If ye have felt to sing the song of redeeming love . . . can ye feel so now?" (Alma 5:26) If you've kept a record of being born again, it'll be an inspiring rebirth story every time you read it.

The scriptures are basically personal journals, and Latter-day Saints are encouraged to keep journals. Here's what Spencer W. Kimball had to say about it:

> On a number of occasions I have encouraged the Saints to keep personal journals and family records. I renew that admonition. We may think there is little of interest or importance in what we personally say or do—but it is remarkable how many of our families, as we pass on down the line, are interested in all that we do and all that we say.
>
> Any Latter-day Saint family that has searched genealogical and historical records has fervently wished its ancestors had kept better and more complete records. On the other hand, some families possess

some spiritual treasures because ancestors have recorded the events surrounding their conversion to the gospel and other happenings of interest, including many miraculous blessings and spiritual experiences. People often use the excuse that their lives are uneventful and nobody would be interested in what they have done. But I promise you that if you will keep your journals and records, they will indeed be a source of great inspiration to your families, to your children, your grandchildren, and others, on through the generations. Each of us is important to those who are near and dear to us—and as our posterity read of our life's experiences, they, too, will come to know and love us. And in that glorious day when our families are together in the eternities, we will already be acquainted.[1]

Learn to Be a Redactor

Remember, you're a redactor, just like Mormon, and at the end of the day you must choose what is important. Rather than simply record the day's events in your journal, you might ask yourself things like, "How did the Spirit manifest itself in my life today? What did I learn today? What interesting thing happened in my relationships that might be useful to record?"

You should allow your personal journal to be just that—personal, but it should also be worth sharing. Put a little writing into it. And maybe, if you are reaching those later decades in life, you might want to do some cutting and pasting and make one really great journal from the many you have on hand. (When President Kimball was sustained as the president of the Church, his journal was already thirty-three volumes in length[2]—help!) If you have been a copious journal writer, some redacting might be in order.

Deliver Up the Record

If you are a talented scrapbooker, you can learn something from Mormon, who knew how to choose the better part as he made his record. And don't forget to bring spiritual substance to your family records.

And if, like me, you're pretty hopeless at it, take courage from the fact that as far as we know, there were no stickers or borders on the plates. As long as you keep a record of the most important things in your family history, you'll be creating a treasure, even if there isn't a border or a sticker on it.

Remember that the most important keepsakes in any family are the keepsakes of the heart and soul: our testimonies, our personal experiences with the Lord, the miracles we have witnessed, and the happiness that comes as a result.

By his masterful redaction of hundreds of years of history, Mormon showed how to choose the better part in our own personal books of life. Someday, each of us will die, and our relations will go through those cupboards and drawers and decide what to keep and what to throw away. Let's be sure we leave them a record of "the things of [our] soul" (2 Nephi 4:15).

How Did Joseph Smith Translate the Book of Mormon?

From first-hand accounts by Emma Smith and various scribes, it appears that the actual process of translation was quite different than the traditional paintings portraying a smiling Joseph Smith in a clean white shirt sitting in front of the golden plates, translating word by word.

In fact, according to Richard Bushman, a more accurate term for the process that Joseph went through would be *transcription* rather than *translation*.[3]

In the original attempt at translation with Martin Harris as scribe, Joseph sat separated by a blanket with the plates open in front of him. Then, after the loss of the 116 pages of manuscript, Joseph resumed the project in April of 1829 with the help of his wife, Emma.

By that time, he had ceased looking at the plates while translating, instead looking into a seerstone (placed in a hat so that it was in a darkened area), upon which he could see about twenty to thirty words at a time. He would dictate these, wait for Emma (or later Oliver Cowdery) to take them down, and then dictate the next passage. Scribes reported that Joseph would dictate without backing up or asking to have lines repeated.

The Book of Mormon is a complex narrative with numerous intersecting plot lines. The fact that the entire volume was all dictated in around three months with no significant corrections is really quite remarkable. Surprisingly, the narrative was not dictated in order, for after the loss of the 116 pages of manuscript Joseph didn't begin the translation over, but rather went on from where he had left off, starting with what is now called the Book of Mosiah. It was only after the translation was finished that he went back (in May or June of 1829) and dictated the first part of the narrative again, covering the first four hundred years of Nephite history.

Clearly, however one views the origin of the Book of Mormon, the historical record shows that it was something that came to Joseph all together and wasn't a carefully constructed narrative cobbled together from various sources. Joseph's recorded sermons are remarkable for how little he refers to or quotes passages from the Book of Mormon, though he often bore solemn testimony of its divine origin. This is more consistent with someone who has transcribed a manuscript than composed one.

Later in life, Joseph Smith's son Joseph Smith III asked his mother if Joseph could have written the manuscript using any texts available at the time. She responded that Joseph at the time "could neither write nor dictate a coherent and well-worded letter; let alone dictating a book like the Book of Mormon. . . . He had neither [manuscripts] nor book to read from. . . . If he had had anything of the kind he could not have concealed it from me." She said she often felt the plates, which were kept under a linen cloth on her kitchen table, and moved them when needed. Emma was his first convert and never recanted her testimony that the plates were real or that the transcription process was divinely inspired. She claimed that the whole thing was "marvelous to her."[4]

Notes

1. Spencer W. Kimball, "President Kimball Speaks Out on Personal Journals," *New Era*, December 1980.

2. Ibid.

3. Richard L. Bushman, "Interview with Emma Smith," *Joseph Smith: Rough Stone Rolling* (New York: Alfred Knopf, 2005).

4. Ibid.

Your Stories and Thoughts

Mosiah: Creating a Culture of Faith

How to Teach Gospel Doctrine, by King Benjamin (Mosiah 1–5)

Let's do a little Mormon math and estimate that over the course of a good, long Latter-day Saint life, you'll attend church fifty weeks a year for seventy years. That's 10,500 hours of church (if you stay for the whole three hours each week). So we're talking about hearing at least 3,500 Sunday School lessons, along with an equal number of priesthood or Relief Society lessons, in addition to the sermons preached in sacrament meeting. That's a lot of lessons! And because we have no paid ministry, most of us will teach some of those lessons along the way.

Out of all those thousands of hours of instruction, what stands out in your memory? Who are the best teachers you've ever had, and what was their teaching method? The Book of Mormon offers us some great examples of teachers and preachers, but none in my opinion equal King Benjamin. Let's take a close look at how to teach a great lesson from his marvelous final discourse.

I notice six crucial components of King Benjamin's success: He set up the physical environment properly, offered people a new way of looking at things, let his own unique personality shine through, asked challenging questions, taught pure doctrine focused on Jesus Christ, and offered specific ways to take action.

Physical environment. King Benjamin had an important message he wanted everyone in the kingdom to hear. So he invited them to come, as families, and placed them strategically, "every man having his tent with the door thereof towards the temple, that thereby they might remain in their tents and hear the words" (Mosiah 2:6).

They couldn't all fit inside, so by them facing toward the temple, King Benjamin created a sacred space that was like an extension of the temple itself. The physical setting already let people know that a special event was about to take place. But King Benjamin was a practical man too. He knew that if people didn't hear the message, they wouldn't feel the Spirit. So he gave his address, and then caused it to be written down and distributed.

I have taught many classes in many settings; without hesitation, the strongest advice I'd give any teacher is to make sure that everyone in your class can see and hear you! Once you are sure of that, prepare your physical surroundings to lead toward the type of experience you wish to create. If you want lots of discussion, sit in a circle. If you want a lecture, provide a way to take notes. Think about what you want to have happen and set up accordingly.

A new vision. A great teacher takes the things we see around us every day and provides a fresh perspective on them. As King Benjamin described it, "I have not commanded you to come up hither to trifle with the words which I shall speak, but that you should hearken unto me, and open your ears that ye may hear, and your hearts that ye may understand, and your minds that the mysteries of God may be unfolded to your view" (Mosiah 2:9).

King Benjamin realized that his people had grown complacent about the commandments and were unwilling to reach out to the poor and suffering among them. But rather than scolding, he began by talking about his own service on their behalf. He truly had given his life in the service of others, so he was in a position to talk about this subject, and they knew it.

As a teacher, the opening and the closing of a lesson are crucial. You have an opportunity to open the ears, hearts, and minds of your audience by engaging their attention and imaginations. You can open their hearts, as King Benjamin did, by recounting something that touches them deeply. Whatever you choose as your opening, think about opening ears, hearts, and minds before you get to "shoulds" and "shouldn'ts."

Let the real you shine through. Nearly everyone is interesting in person, but not many people are interesting as speakers or teachers. This is often because people are afraid to let their personalities shine in lessons and talks. They say what they think they should say, read a few safe quotes, and repeat the same maxims that have been repeated countless times. Why do we do this? People love it when a teacher brings something different, something unique. I recently attended a Gospel Doctrine class where the teacher, Heber Crockett, taught the class all about pitching: how fast the pitch moves, how many bones and muscles are involved, how little time the batter has to make a decision, and how the batter can't even see the ball once the swing begins! As a former pitcher, Heber had a personal connection to the sport, and, though he made a great gospel application from it, it was his enthusiasm for the baseball facts that drew us all in. We all learned something that we wouldn't have learned from anyone else, and we loved getting to know our teacher better as well.

A great moment in American history illustrates this point. George Washington was an outstanding leader but, by most accounts, he was not an inspiring speaker. At a crucial time in the Revolutionary War, many of his troops and their officers were about to abandon the fight. Washington wanted to give an inspiring speech to win back their support. He stood up to speak, and there was an embarrassed silence as he began to fumble in his pocket for his spectacles. In exasperation, he looked up and reportedly said, "I have not only grown gray but almost blind in the service of my country."[1] Though he was an intensely private man who didn't like to show weakness, this unguarded moment had the most powerful effect on his officers. Several wept openly as they looked upon their humble leader and thought about the sacrifices he had made for years. Dropping that wall for a moment and allowing people to see a weak and vulnerable man instead of only a commander won the day for Washington, as nearly all of his officers chose to stay and fight to the end with him.

Ask challenging questions. King Benjamin's address started with several thought-provoking questions: "If I, whom ye call your king, do labor to serve you, then ought not ye to labor to serve one another?" (Mosiah 2:18). "Therefore, of what have ye to boast? And now I ask, can ye say aught of yourselves?" (Mosiah 2:24–25).

While teaching, have you ever asked questions that no one seemed willing to answer? For example, "Who appeared to Joseph Smith in the Sacred Grove?" The class just stares at you, and you grow frustrated. Why won't anyone answer such a simple question? Well, perhaps people feel shy about answering specific questions in front of a group—what if they are wrong? Or perhaps they feel that the question is too simple, so they just don't bother answering it. A great teacher asks open-ended questions that cause people to think. Rather than ask, "Who appeared to Joseph Smith?" you might instead ask, "Why would God choose a fourteen-year-old boy to receive the First Vision?" Open-ended thought-provoking questions are hard to prepare but well worth the effort. I consider them the most important part of a lesson.

Teach pure doctrine, centered in Christ. Of all of the things King Benjamin could have spoken about in his last address, he chose to focus on Jesus. The Atonement, mission, and life of Jesus Christ is the one thing really worth talking about. It is the good news, for its message "healeth the wounded soul" (Jacob 2:8). When you prepare a lesson, it should be like preparing a good meal, with the biggest portion of the plate being devoted to the most nourishing food: the living bread and water that is the Savior. Rules, regulations, and doctrinal details are like starches and sweets—a little goes a long way. If you need to talk about sins or preach repentance, do so sparingly. The greatest reason people come to church is to feel the encouraging, healing Spirit of the Lord, and that Spirit comes when we talk about Christ. So don't get mired in the details; get to Jesus.

I served as the stake president for the Young Women for about three years; during that time, I spoke to hundreds of girls and their leaders. Just for fun, I made a private goal that during my tenure I would never tell anyone what she shouldn't do. Instead, I would just try to talk about the Savior and His grace and mercy and suggest all the positive things everyone could do as a result of His Atonement.

It's so easy, especially with the youth, to focus on things we shouldn't do. Though it's important to be clear about standards, it can all get to be a bit much. So I decided that the youth in the stake had enough people telling them what they shouldn't do, so I'd just focus on the opportunities and blessings that came from our faith. It was a joyful time for me, and it made me aware of how many times we try to use negative remarks to achieve a positive result. King Benjamin showed that if you're going to talk about negative behavior (which he does), you had better follow it by preaching Jesus and His redeeming grace in a big way, or people will go away discouraged.

Suggest specific ways to act. King Benjamin's address had a pretty impressive result: his people "viewed themselves in their own carnal state" (Mosiah 4:2). Poet Robert Burns said, "Oh the gift that God would give us, to see ourselves as others see us."[2] Self-knowledge is rare; we usually see ourselves quite inaccurately and need the Spirit to help us see who and what we really are. When these people saw themselves clearly, they actually fell to the earth and cried with one voice, "O have mercy, and apply the atoning blood of Christ that we may receive forgiveness of our sins" (Mosiah 4:2).

Now that he had them where he wanted them, King Benjamin helped his people take action. Renaming them children of Christ, he led them in making a covenant with the Savior, and then took them into a step-by-step tutorial on the Christian life. He realized that they would have had neither the will nor the inclination to change their behavior without the influence of the Holy Spirit, but now that it had been poured out in a Pentecostal degree, anything was possible. So he used that golden moment to commit them to action. Missionaries are really good at this; they are trained to inspire people to act. Have an end in mind for your lesson: What do you want people to do as a result of it? Aim for it. And when you get that spirit, suggest specific ways to act.

It Can Happen to You

Let's review the teaching techniques here. King Benjamin gathered his people and created a sacred space for a meeting. He had two objectives: to testify of the Savior and to inspire his people to take better care of each other. He began by opening his own life to his listeners and getting them to feel grateful for all of the service they have received from him. Then he painted a vision of how every person there was, in fact, a beggar, just like the ones they passed on the way in. He then set up the challenge of caring for the less fortunate. Once the group sensed their unworthiness, King Benjamin preached about Jesus Christ with all the vigor he had, showing how his service as a king was nothing compared to the gift of the Atonement. He knew that this was the only subject that changes hearts. Finally, when he saw that they were filled with the Spirit, he led them in taking action as they covenanted to become Christians.

Can you have your own King Benjamin experiences in your teaching? I believe you can. The Spirit of the Lord is always available, and people desperately need and want to be touched by it—that's why they come to church. You can be the conduit for bringing Jesus into a classroom. Don't send them away hungry and thirsty; instead, create an environment where they feel invigorated and filled. Set your room up so that everyone can hear and see and sense a sacred experience is at hand. Open with a creative story or concept that sheds new light on something familiar and engages their interest. Allow your listeners to see into your life a little. Ask open-ended thought-provoking questions that help people see themselves as they really are. Teach pure doctrine, centered in Jesus Christ.

And then, when the Spirit is strong, suggest concrete ways to implement the principles you've discussed. Take King Benjamin as a model and, with the Lord's help, you will create a situation where your class responds, "It is the faith which we have had on the things which our [teacher] has spoken unto us that has brought us to this great knowledge, whereby we do rejoice with such exceedingly great joy" (Mosiah 5:4).

There are some great examples of chiasmus in Mosiah. Here's one from King Benjamin's sermon in Mosiah 5:10–12:

a Whosoever shall not take upon him the *name of Christ*
  b must be *called* by some other name;
    c therefore, he findeth himself on the *left hand of God*.
      d And I would that ye should *remember* also, that this is the name . . .
        e that never should be *blotted out*,
          f except it be through *transgression*;
          therefore,
          f take heed that ye do not *transgress*,
        e that the name be not *blotted out* of your hearts . . .
      d I would that ye should *remember* to retain the name . . .
    c that ye are not found on the *left hand of God*,
  b but that ye hear and know the voice by which ye shall be *called*,
a and also, the *name* by which he shall call you.[3]

The Parable of the Prophet, Priest, and King (Mosiah 11–18)

Once there was a man named Noah, who was chosen by his father to succeed him as king. He got off to a bad start by getting rid of all of the righteous priests who had counseled his father, surrounding himself instead with "such as were lifted up in the pride of their hearts" (Mosiah 11:5). He slapped a 20 percent tax on his people and squandered it on himself and his entourage. "And thus they were supported in their laziness, and in their idolatry, and in their whoredoms, by the taxes which king Noah had put upon his people; thus did the people labor exceedingly to support iniquity" (Mosiah 11:6).

One day, however, King Noah met his match with Abinadi, a prophet who came among the people and fearlessly preached repentance. When Abinadi warned Noah of God's coming judgments, the king had him arrested. There, surrounded by his wicked advisors, Noah threatened Abinadi with death. But Abinadi stood and delivered a great sermon on Jesus Christ and His mission. It seemed that no one was listening, but Abinadi didn't care; he had a message to deliver, and he did so with such power and authority that he almost frightened the wicked king into letting him go. But, in the end, the king sentenced Abinadi to die, who passed on without ever seeing any successful outcome for his efforts.

Unbeknownst to Abinadi and King Noah, however, there was a third character in this drama—a young priest named Alma, who had somehow managed to fly below the radar and escape the king's notice. Alma was so moved by Abinadi's message that he pled for Abinadi's life before the king, causing Noah to turn on Alma and even send servants to slay him. Alma fled into the night and hid; after writing down all the words of the prophet, Alma taught them to the people. Eventually, a whole group of faithful Christians grew from that one small seed of faith, planted by a prophet just before giving his life for the truth.

This is an encouraging story for missionaries because Abinadi has only one convert. (We aren't told whether they actually even interacted or whether Abinadi was even present at the time that Alma pled for Abinadi's life.) This one convert, however, became the nexus of a great Christian movement, transforming the history of the Nephites.

The story inspires every missionary or teacher who feels like no one is listening, reminding us that God has a greater plan and our little efforts may bear fruit one day.

It's a great and inspiring story. But what if we look at the story in another way? What if we also see it as a parable about one person? What if inside every one of us there is a King Noah, an Abinadi, and an Alma? How does that drama play out?

The Bad News: I'm King Noah

Though it's uncomfortable to admit, each of us has elements of the wicked King Noah in us, don't we? Noah is lazy, idolatrous, and unchaste. We are all tempted in such directions and may succumb now and then in large or small ways. When we do, we tend to do as Noah did—that is, we surround ourselves with friends and flatterers who agree with our points of view and do not tell us the truth. (This kind of behavior is, of course, much easier to see in other, really sinful people, but we all do it to a certain extent.)

Our close friends tend to be people who share our viewpoints and behavior levels and do not make us uneasy by urging us to do better. If my language is a little rough, I'm attracted to others with the same weakness. If I'm casual about Sabbath observance, I'm more comfortable with others who act the same way. If I'm skeptical about certain policies of the Church, I tend to group myself with others who have the same viewpoint. This is quite "natural"—and you know what the scriptures say about the "natural man" (see Mosiah 3:19).

How we love nice things! King Noah loved luxury. (He probably was at the lot buying the latest chariot as soon as they came out every year.) He spent lots of money on his palace and even upgraded the temple furnishings so that his seat (now made of pure gold) and those of his priests were high above the others; in fact, they were shielded from others by a breastwork "that they might rest their bodies and their arms upon while they should speak lying and vain words to his people" (Mosiah 11:11). Noah really represents the extreme of everything we don't want to be, so it's easy to dismiss him as completely unlike ourselves.

Well, I don't know about you, but I can see a little of myself in this guy. I really don't like to hear criticism about myself; I much prefer when people tell me how great I am. The priesthood holder sneaking a look at porn or the Relief Society teacher making fun of the bishop resemble him a little. We've all got some wickedness in us that needs to be eradicated, and most of us spend quite a bit of energy avoiding the voices that would tell us the specific ways we need to repent. Why? Because, like Noah and his priests, we are lazy. It's hard work to repent, and we would just as soon avoid it. But once I recognize that there's a bit of King Noah in me, I can also observe the way he responds to the voice of the prophet Abinadi, and I can try to guard against his type of angry, defensive behavior.

Come Listen to a Prophet's Voice

Abinadi represents the voice of God speaking through his prophets, in the scriptures and in our hearts. When that voice comes to us, how do we respond? One insightful teacher recently described the way we make little "carve outs" for ourselves in the gospel plan. He explained that even as we listen to lessons and talks, we are often busy excusing any behavior that is in opposition to the gospel standards with a list of reasons why that particular commandment doesn't apply to us. For example, we may say to ourselves, *Yeah, we need to keep the Sabbath day holy, but to be too strict about it just shows that we don't get the higher point, which is to be loving and serve others. So as long as I do that, it doesn't matter if I shop or go out to eat on a Sunday.* We conveniently "carve out" a little comfort zone so that certain commandments don't have to apply to us.[4]

What we may not realize, however, is how our actions impact others. King Noah and his priests spoke "flattering things" to the people and actually persuaded them to labor to "support [the] iniquity" of their leaders (Mosiah 5:6–7). If instead they had been setting a righteous example (as King Benjamin was for his people), they could have been such a force for good. Often, it isn't whether one action is intrinsically bad; it is the effect of that action upon the faith of those around us we must examine. Jacob said, "Because of your bad examples before them . . . the sobbings of their hearts ascend up to God against you" (Jacob 2:35). We are judged both by our actions and by the example we set to others. Like King Noah, each of us has people who are influenced by our actions, and if we cause others to "support [our iniquities]," we will be accountable for that.

So how do we respond when our Abinadi—maybe a Church leader, spouse, or even one of our children—calls us to repentance? Do we shield ourselves (as with a breastwork) with excuses, anger, or defensive behaviors? Do we shut that person out of our lives? For example, do we just listen to the conference speakers who appeal to us and avoid those that seem too strict? Do we discount the counsel we receive by focusing on the imperfections of the leaders who offer it? All of these reactions are natural, but again, we know what the scriptures say about the natural man.

We need the power of God to see ourselves, not through a glass darkly, but as we really are (see 1 Corinthians 13:12). Noah refused to do this, and when Abinadi told Noah the truth about him, Noah responded with anger and almost breathtaking conceit, "Who is Abinadi, that I and my people should be judged of him, or who is the Lord, that shall bring upon my people such great affliction?" (Mosiah 11:27).

As Abinadi continued to bear down in pure testimony—and even placed the curse of his innocent blood squarely on the king's head—Noah had the next "natural" response: fear. He "feared that the judgments of God would come upon him" and wanted to let Abinadi go (Mosiah 17:11). But his entourage (undoubtedly fearing the end of the gravy train they'd been riding for a few years), flattered him back into that first reaction of anger and pride, and Abinadi suffered a martyr's death at Noah's command.

The Good News: I'm Alma

In case we're getting too discouraged, this parable has a bright side; for within each of us, there is also a young Alma. This is the open, eternally hopeful part of our spirits that responds to truth with joy and courage. When the word of the prophet comes to us, it kindles a light in our hearts that is just waiting to turn into a burning fire.

We respond enthusiastically to the truth, as Alma did, writing "all the words which Abinadi had spoken" (Mosiah 17:4). Then "[he] repented of his sins and iniquities . . . and began to teach the words of Abinadi" (Mosiah 18:1).

Can you imagine the personal cost to Alma, deciding to follow the bright, shining part of his spirit rather than the dark, self-serving side? Remember, he shared in the wealth that the 20 percent tax brought to the priests. He was one of the king's favored few; he had great power and (I'm sure) a luxurious lifestyle. If he ignored Abinadi, he wouldn't have to repent or change his ways. And, perhaps most of all, he never had to look squarely at himself and admit that his life was on a completely wrong course. Simply by shielding himself, as the others did, from the words of the prophet, Alma could have continued on a comfortable, carnal path.

But Alma had something great inside that leaped up when he heard the truth. I have often heard people say, "I don't know where I would be today without the gospel." Though I'm among the weakest of the Saints, I know exactly where I would be today without the gospel: I'd be looking for it! I think this is true of most of us. If we didn't have the gospel, we would be searching for it, because there is something within us that responds with joy, as Alma did when he heard it preached.

In one of the great moments in the scriptures, Alma (who appeared to be the only one with priesthood authority) baptized himself and one of the first responders to his message at the same time, "and they arose and came forth out of the water rejoicing, being filled with the Spirit" (Mosiah 18:14).

Three in One

Three is a special number in God's kingdom. Just as there are three members of the Godhead, we have three elements inside ourselves: the wicked and carnal side, the joyful and righteous side, and (in the middle) the voice of God speaking through our consciences. In a wrenching reflection of our own hearts, Christ hung on the cross between two thieves. One of the thieves thought only of himself right to the end. The other used the moments he spent next to Christ to see himself as he truly was, accept the consequences of his sin, and pray for forgiveness.

When the voice of God comes to us through the scriptures, our leaders, or the whisperings of the Holy Spirit, will we behave like King Noah (and the first thief), responding with defensiveness, anger and fear? Or will we respond like Alma (and the second thief) and repent of our sins and iniquities?

The fact that we're reading and studying God's word and trying to come to grips with our own sins and failings gives us hope that there is far more of Alma than Noah in each of us. But understanding that each of us does have that wicked, self-serving side is essential to becoming whole. Before we can be healed, we need to know we are in need of the Master Physician.

The only way for us to overcome that wicked King Noah is to place ourselves completely in the hands of the Savior, acknowledging that we have, at best, only a fuzzy view of ourselves as we really are. Samuel Beckett (inspired by Saint Augustine) reminded us neither to think too much nor too little of ourselves: "Do not despair; one of the thieves was saved. Do not presume; one of the thieves was damned."[5] The only answer, then, is to throw our lives on the mercy of the great Being in the center, as He alone has power to save us from ourselves and take us with Him into eternal life.

Ordinary People with Extraordinary Lives

The ancient Hebrews were comfortable with the idea that their leaders were human, and so the Bible features characters with both strengths and flaws. If we simply assume that everything a prophet does represents the ideal choice in any given situation, we are simply lumping them into one pile labeled "perfect people who are nothing like me." Thus we may miss opportunities to find ourselves in the narrative.

There are significant differences in these great prophets, such as their personalities, temperaments, and ways of handling challenges. Nephi was a incredibly different person from Alma, who was in turn remarkably different from Moroni. We may or may not agree with all of their choices, but it is illuminating to think about, for example, Alma's parenting style as compared with Lehi's, or King Benjamin's leadership style versus Moroni's.

The Baptismal Covenant: Six Steps to Becoming a Christian (Mosiah 18)

We know that Alma (the quiet priest who sat in the corner and took notes while Abinadi testified his life away) escaped from King Noah and his wicked cohorts and "went about privately among the people, and began to teach the words of Abinadi. . . . And many did believe his words" (Mosiah 18:1, 3).

Noah's high taxes and riotous lifestyle surely would have created a fertile ground of discontent in which Alma could sow his gospel seeds. Soon, crowds gathered to hear the young priest, but he was not preaching political revolution. Instead, what they heard from Alma was revolution of a deeper sort, consisting of "repentance, and redemption, and faith on the Lord" (Mosiah 18:7).

Left to interpret the words of Abinadi for himself, Alma settled on his own definition of a Christian and listed six qualifications necessary for baptism. To be worthy, one must be desirous to come into the fold of God; desirous to be called His people; willing to bear one another's burdens; willing to mourn with those who mourn; willing to comfort those who stand in need of comfort; and willing to stand as witnesses of God at all times, in all things, and in all places that you may be until death (see Mosiah 18:8–9).

Desirous to come into the fold. Latter-day Saints really believe in the importance of the Church. In fact, we believe that we are members of the church to which everyone ought to belong—the true Church of Christ. As a missionary in Japan, I found quite a cultural and linguistic disconnect occurred when I testified to people that the Church was true. Though too polite to argue with me, this statement was invariably met with blank looks. Finally, a candid Japanese person said to me, "I understand how a statement can be true and even a doctrine. But a church can no more be true than a building or a piano can be true. It is an organization. It is a constructed thing. How can a thing be true?"

Good question! What then do we mean when we say that the Church is true? We mean, of course, that it is the repository of true doctrines and ordinances required for salvation. We also mean that it

The User-Friendly Book of Mormon

is proper or correct in its organization and authority. But I think we mean something more as well when we use this phrase—something that is harder to articulate. In the way, we might call someone who looks and acts in an ideally masculine way a *real man*, so when we call it a *true church*, we mean that the Church is truly what a church *should be*. It looks and acts like the true Church should look and act.

In his book of the same name, Eugene England wrote a brilliant essay titled "Why the Church Is as True as the Gospel." Using his faithful service as anecdotal evidence, he countered an expression among Saints that, though the gospel is true, the Church isn't quite "true" because it's a human, history-bound thing, and thus imperfect. He wrote, "I am persuaded by experiences . . . and by my best thinking that, in fact, the Church is as 'true,' as effective, as sure an instrument of salvation as the system of doctrines we call the gospel—and that is so in good part because of the very flaws, human exasperations, and historical problems that occasionally give us all some anguish."[6]

England went on to give several really moving examples of how the Church creates a "school of love,"[7] in which we are required to practice Christian virtues of compassion, patience, courage, and discipline. Connected by our membership to a group of people with whom we might not otherwise choose to associate—let alone love— we are in turn challenged, stretched, disappointed, and exasperated, as well as served, inspired, and strengthened. And thus we grow into Christians in deed and belief. A willingness to step into this group is part of being a Christian. Without a desire "to come into the fold," you are just theorizing (Mosiah 18:8).

Desirous to be called His people. I'm sure that Mormon would've been surprised to learn that we would eventually be known by his name rather than identified as Christians. It is a shame, and perhaps one of the first steps toward being recognized as Christians by the world is for Latter-day Saints to start calling themselves by Christ's name, not just Mormon's. The Church is named for Christ, and we should be as well. Would it seem strange to introduce ourselves as Latter-day Saint Christians? I haven't quite worked this out for myself yet, but it seems to be an important distinction to make right from the start, that we are followers of Christ. We admire Mormon, but we worship Jesus.

Author C. S. Lewis reminded us that true Christians are not just the saintly, robed figures in the scriptures; they are all around us: "Our model is the Jesus, not only of Calvary, but of the workshop, the roads, the crowds, the clamorous demands and surly oppositions, the lack of all peace and privacy, the interruptions. For this, so strangely unlike anything we can attribute to the Divine life in itself, is apparently not only like, but is, the Divine life operating under human conditions."[8]

Willing to bear one another's burdens. What does this mean? For Joseph Smith, it was more than a spiritual goal; it meant setting up a Zion society, where people had all things in common. We are apparently not ready to do that, but we certainly are told over and over again in the Book of Mormon that we are responsible, both body and soul, for the welfare of our fellow humans. We pay one tenth of our increase in a tithe, but many of us still have so much. How should we share?

For one of my professors, this meant that he kept his pockets full of change to hand to any beggars he might pass. For some of our friends, it meant adopting five children from Africa in addition to their own five. For one dentist I know, it meant treating so many patients for free that I wondered how his practice thrived. Bearing the burdens of others will manifest itself in different ways in each life, but the willingness should always be there.

There is a sobering message at the end of Matthew 25 when Jesus gave the parable of the sheep and the goats. Notice how it begins:

> When the Son of man shall come in his glory, and all the holy angels with him, then shall he sit upon the throne of his glory: and before him shall be gathered all nations: and he shall separate them one from another, as a shepherd divideth his sheep from the goats: and he shall set the sheep on his right hand, but the goats on the left. Then shall the King say unto them on his right hand, Come, ye blessed of my Father, inherit the kingdom prepared for you from the foundation of the world: for I was an hungred, and ye gave me meat: I was thirsty, and ye gave me drink: I was a stranger, and ye took me in: naked, and ye clothed me: I was sick, and ye visited me: I was in prison, and ye came unto me. (Matthew 25:31–36)

Jesus wasn't just talking about individuals; he was talking about nations. Won't it be interesting if, on Judgment Day, God cares less about how many wars we won, instead asking the leaders of nations to report how they fared in this requirement of bearing the burdens of the suffering, the hungry, the imprisoned, and the sick. How will the leaders of nations, and the citizens who voted on laws, fare when judged on these simple criteria?

Only Jesus can teach us how to translate this injunction into our modern lives, but it doesn't do any good to try to separate our gospel beliefs from the down-and-dirty details of daily life. We must decide what to do about the beggars, the people on welfare, and the neighborhoods into which we normally would not venture, because we will be asked later what we did to carry the love of Christ into every corner of our moral proximity. Christ was never a God reserved for Sunday; He was involved in every detail of life. Rabbi Harold Kushner said, "The voice that commands us to volunteer our time at a homeless shelter, the voice that urges us to put the needs and feelings of our family ahead of our own, is the voice of God, because those are things we are unlikely to have thought of on our own."[9]

Mourn with those who mourn; comfort those who stand in need of comfort. The abysmal performance of Job's "comforters" reminds us that comforting is a skill more talked about than really practiced. Well-meaning versions of comforting can range from thoughtless comments that cause more pain ("God is testing you because He loves you" or "If you had more faith, this could have been avoided") to a kind of can-you-top-this conversation that lists worse cases ("I'm so sorry about your miscarriage, but I know a woman who has had five of them") to an avoidance of the whole situation that makes the sufferer feel discounted and ignored. (One little girl reported how, after her father died, her friends just stopped talking to her because they didn't know what to say.)

Effective comforting is a skill; it can be learned, and the willingness to learn is a godly desire, because the Holy Ghost and Jesus are the ultimate Comforters. To learn this skill, we can think about the ways God offers comfort, read examples, pray about it, and then practice. Effective comforting is quiet, personal, and tailored to each individual. But there is a key to getting it right, and I discovered it one time when I was doing an especially clumsy job of comforting someone who really needed it. The key is to tap into the source.

As a young wife and mother, my worst nightmare was realized in the life of a friend when she lost her husband suddenly in a freak accident, leaving her with three young children and no means of support. In one day, she went from being a happy, successful woman to a bereaved, broken one. I was assigned to take the family a meal, and this was the easy part; I could pour all of my sympathy into a baked ham, potatoes, rolls, and salad, and I could pack it all up in a basket and take it to the house. But once I got there, I couldn't bring myself to get out of the car. I sat across the street, frightened to go to the door. I was afraid of the pain on the other side of that door, of the raw need of that young mom and her fatherless children. And, to be honest, I was afraid of the way her loss made me feel—vulnerable to tragedy as well, as if I might somehow "catch" it from her. I just wanted to leave the basket on the doorstep and run.

Finally, ashamed of myself, I worked up my courage, went up to the front door, and knocked. The door opened and, almost in a perceptible rush, the Spirit flowed out to me. There stood this lovely woman, tearful yet smiling, and as she gathered me into her arms, I felt how the Holy Spirit, maybe even the Savior Himself, was there with all of them in the room. I was loved, hugged, thanked, and welcomed. Those who stood in need of comfort comforted me. I went away, humbled and amazed at "the grace that so fully he proffers" every soul in need of it.[10]

Later, I wondered how I could've hesitated, even feared to go to that door. Didn't I know who was on the other side? Of course I was lonely and afraid in the car; I wasn't the one who was suffering, and how many times has Jesus told us that where there is suffering, it is there we will find Him? I finally understood then what my beautiful cousin Kay means when she says, "I love to be near new babies and also to go to funerals because I know in both cases that angels are there." Learning to step up and offer comfort is to step into the presence of the Comforter Himself. It's not a burden; it's a glorious privilege because it allows us to tap into the greatest source of comfort in the universe.

Willing to stand as witnesses of God at all times, in all things, and in all places. Let's face it, it can be kind of embarrassing to be religious. It's never been cool or popular, from the days of Noah to our day. It was meant to be that way. Lehi saw a great and spacious building where people were pointing and laughing at the righteous, making them feel embarrassed and ashamed of holding onto the simple iron rod and plodding forward in faith. So they hesitated, stumbled, and let go. This business of ridicule is effective—people are letting go all the time. The reasons for laughing and mocking vary through the ages, but the effectiveness remains. Nobody likes to look silly, so it's easier just to let go of faith and "go with the flow."

Standing as a witness of God at all times, in all things, and in all places is really hard, and it's especially hard to do it without completely annoying everyone you know! I love a *New Yorker* cartoon that shows a plump, smiling woman with a cross around her neck and a Bible in her hand sitting on a bus next to a wary-looking stranger. The caption has her saying, "I find the ride goes a lot quicker when you have someone to try to convert."

How do we know when to witness, when to be quiet, or when to take some position in between those two extremes? Once again, we aren't alone in this effort. Christ showed examples of all three behaviors and more, and He can teach us how to respond in each situation. Whether it was to kneel and write in the sand as a woman was condemned and afterward speak to her privately or to braid a cord and storm through the temple courtyards turning over tables, Jesus did what was needed when it was needed to let people know He lived for God's cause, not for His own.

Whatever the case, in my experience, the Lord will consistently find ways to surprise us, as He did so often in His brief ministry. I love this beautiful poem about the way our lives turn wonderfully upside down when we take Him in and how the only way to describe His behavior and His love is "boundless":

> You take a risk when you invite the Lord
> Whether to dine or talk the afternoon
> Away, for always the unexpected soon
> Turns up: a woman breaks her precious nard,
> A sinner does the task you should assume,

A leper who is cleansed must show his proof:
Suddenly you see your very roof removed
And a cripple clutters up your living room.
There's no telling what to expect when Christ
Walks in your door. The table set for four
Must often be enlarged and decorum
Thrown to the wind. It's His voice that calls them
And it's no use to bolt and bar the door:
His kingdom knows no bounds of roof, or wall, or floor.[11]

Alma and his followers took a real risk when they formed a group and called themselves Christians, yet as we read, we feel is the joy that filled their souls when they found a hope and home in Christ.

And hundreds of years later, the lonely man telling the story (who had been named for the beautiful scene of their conversion) couldn't restrain himself from expressing the joy that he knew they felt in that moment; he felt it as he chiseled their story into the sacred record: "And now it came to pass that all this was done in Mormon, yea, by the waters of Mormon, in the forest that was near the waters of Mormon; yea, the place of Mormon, the waters of Mormon, the forest of Mormon, how beautiful are they to the eyes of them who there came to the knowledge of their Redeemer; yea, and how blessed are they, for they shall sing to his praise forever" (Mosiah 18:30).

The Alma Family: Control versus Influence Parenting (Mosiah 27)

One of the most fascinating parent-child relationships in the Book of Mormon is that of Alma the Elder and Alma the Younger, as they are known. Alma the Elder was one of King Noah's priests. He heard Abinadi preach, was converted, escaped the king's wrath, and started his own little colony of Christians.

Alma the Younger was thrown together with the princes, who were the sons of King Mosiah, and they were a bad group of guys. They not only rejected everything their fathers had taught them, but they persecuted those who believed. Their story is recounted twice—once in Mormon's third-person narrative in Mosiah 27, and again in Alma the Younger's own voice in a letter to his son Helaman, recorded in Alma 36.

I'm fascinated by Alma's approach to his rebellious son. We don't know all of the details of their relationship, but we do know that the situation was serious. This wasn't a young kid goofing around in the parking lot at church; this was a grown man who inherited his father's gifts of preaching and persuasion and used them to flatter and lead away "many of the people to do after the manner of his iniquities. And he became a great hindrance to the prosperity of the church" (Mosiah 27:8–9).

What's a Parent to Do?

What should Alma the Elder have done? We learn that he was given power to prosecute those who chose to persecute believers. With his own son as the ringleader, several options would have been available to him as a means to control his wicked son. Deciding what to do must have been a terrible conundrum for him.

Our obligation as parents can feel equally confusing at times. We are commanded both to control and influence our children. How does that work in real life?

We have been given an injunction by the Lord to "bring up [our] children in light and truth" (DC 93:40). This is a commandment the Lord takes quite seriously. He warned us that "inasmuch as parents have children in Zion . . . that teach them not to understand the doctrine of repentance, faith in Christ the Son of the living God, and of baptism and the gift of the Holy Ghost by the laying on of the hands, when eight years old, the sin be upon the heads of the parents" (DC 68:25).

This doesn't seem all that hard, does it? Most of our children get baptized and confirmed. But there is another verse attached this, only sixteen words in length, which forms the lifelong challenge that's making many of us a little crazy. Here it is: "And they shall also teach their children to pray, and to walk uprightly before the Lord" (DC 68:28).

That's the tough part isn't it? It's not getting them into the waters of baptism but into a life of faith, prayer, and obedience that's really tough. And it's all because of a "tragic flaw" in the plan—agency. Any mother worth her salt will tell you what a mistake this agency is! Why, we know exactly what our children ought to do, and if we could just force them to do it, everything would be fine. Unfortunately, we know who the author of this kind of plan was, and he's on the other team.

So the first thing we must realize as Christian parents is this: In God's plan, we may influence but not control our children's lives. To think that we can control them is an illusion. When children are young, we do have a certain amount of control; we can use our power as parents to force children to make right choices, and this is a good thing. (There's nothing worse than a parent who is afraid to control a young child, as anyone who has watched *Supernanny* can tell you.) In fact, this scripture indicates that if we do not adequately control our children when they are young, it's a sin. However, there is a limit to our control over our kids—there's even a point at which it becomes a sin to try to compel them to do things.

Control versus Influence

Let's look just a moment at Doctrine and Covenants 121, where the principle of control versus influence is taught. The definitions of these words teach us much. Control, from the Latin roots *con* ("against") and *rotula* ("to roll"), means to push against an opposing force and win. Influence is a really old word that is used to describe a liquid substance flowing into the soul—it is related to the words *fluid* and *fluency*. You can feel the difference in the words—one means to push and force and the other means to change from the inside out. Let's compare the verses:

> The rights of the priesthood are inseparably connected with the powers of heaven. . . . When we undertake to cover our sins, or to gratify our pride, our vain ambition, or to exercise control or dominion or compulsion upon the souls of the children of men, in any degree of unrighteousness, behold, the heavens withdraw themselves; the Spirit of the Lord is grieved; and when it is withdrawn, Amen to the priesthood or the authority of that man [or woman]. (D&C 121:36–37)

> No power or influence can or ought to be maintained by virtue of the priesthood, only by persuasion, by long-suffering, by gentleness and meekness, and by love unfeigned. (D&C 121:41)

We buy CTR rings for our kids; we tell them to choose the right and to remember who they are. But in reality, we know that when our children leave our home for the school day—or to college for the school year, and then leave our homes forever—we can't control the choices they make. As children of God, this is true of us as well. God cannot force us to choose the right. As the hymn says, "This eternal truth is giv'n: / That God will force no man to heav'n."[12] As our children move toward adulthood physically, we are expected to move toward a spiritual adulthood that recognizes the futility and danger of trying to manipulate and control our children, whether with money, criticism, or the withholding of love. If we are trying to exercise control over the lives of our adult children, we lose the priesthood power that is our only chance of saving them.

Alma Chose Active, Faith-Filled Influence

Faced with the choice between control and influence, Alma the Elder chose to influence his son. How did he do this? He went straight to the source and put the matter in the Lord's hands. Many times as parents when we find ourselves unable to control our kids, we figuratively wash our hands of them. We just give up and let them go their own way. But this isn't what Alma chose to do. When an angel appeared in a cloud with a voice of thunder and nearly scared Alma the Younger to death, the angel described how Alma the Elder chose to influence his son: "Behold, the Lord hath heard the prayers of his people, and also the prayers of his servant, Alma, who is thy father; for he has prayed with much faith concerning thee that thou mightest be brought to the knowledge of the truth; therefore, for this purpose have I come to convince thee of the power and authority of God, that the prayers of his servants might be answered according to their faith" (Mosiah 27:14).

Let's look at the elements of influence in this verse: Alma the Elder enlisted the help of the community of believers. He prayed with much faith (probably for many years) for his son to have a change of heart. God answered that prayer with a miracle.

There are many quiet, insidious ways to control a child, and they all involve withholding things. We can withhold love, acceptance, friendship, and money in an attempt to manipulate our kids. We can make them feel that their very lives are a disappointment to us, thus inflicting a kind of emotional torture on them. It's almost impossible not to do some of these things, but in the end, even if we succeed in changing some behaviors, these tactics will never cause a change of heart.

Pray for the Miracle

My wonderful cousin Kay Merrill Richards has been a mentor to me as a mother. She is a modern-day Alma. Her advice, when faced with a wayward child, is to opt for faith in Christ. Here is how she avoids the temptation to try to manipulate a child or to just stew and worry. She says, "When that nagging pain about that child's decisions comes into my heart, I banish fear and worry; instead, I say this, 'In the name of Jesus Christ and by the power of the covenants I have made in the temple, I pray for a miracle to happen in the life of my child.' Day after day, week after week, year after year, we pray for the miracle. And, because Christ is more powerful than fear or evil, the miracle will surely come."

One free-thinking child I know caused his mother to stop and reexamine her attitude when he said, "When will you be able to see my life as a path I was meant to walk instead of a disappointment to your expectations?" Suddenly, she thought, *What if my Savior constantly made me feel like I was disappointing Him?* She thought of how she felt love and acceptance and forgiveness flowing out to her whenever she prayed and how that made her want to continue trying to be close to the Lord. She asked herself, *Is my attitude toward my children one of grace or one of judgment?* This can be a life-changing self-examination for any parent.

If a child must be called to repentance with "a voice of thunder," let the angel do it! Such beings know how to do that kind of thing without destroying the soul. As parents, let's opt for the prayer of faith, coupled with eternal love, and trust in our Savior to bring that child (whether young or adult) into the loving circle of grace in His own way and in His own time.

Notes

1. George Washington, George Washington Prevents the Revolt of His Officers," *The History Place*, http://www.historyplace.com /speeches/washington.htm.

2. Robert Burns, "To a Louse: On Seeing One on a Lady's Bonnet at Church," 1786; modern English translation.

3. John Welch, "Chiasmus in the Book of Mormon," *Book of Mormon Authorship*, edited Noel B. Reynolds (Salt Lake City: Bookcraft, 1982).

4. My thanks to John Alexander for this insight.

5. Samuel Beckett, *Waiting for Godot*, act one; English translation.

6. Eugene England, *Why the Church Is as True as the Gospel* (Salt Lake City: Bookcraft, 1978) 36.

7. Ibid.

8. C. S. Lewis, *The Four Loves* (New York: Harcourt Brace Jovanovich, 1960), 17.

9. Harold S. Kushner, *Living a Life that Matters* (New York: Alfred A. Knopf, 2001), 97.

10. "I Stand All Amazed," *Hymns*, no. 193.

11. Marcella Marie Holloway, "The Risk," *Divine Inspiration: The Life of Jesus in World Poetry*, edited by Robert Atwan, George Dardess, Peggy Rosenthal (New York: Oxford University Press, 1998), 118.

12. "Know This, That Every Soul Is Free," *Hymns*, no. 240.

Your Stories and Thoughts

Alma: Wars Within and Without

Pop Quiz: Is It Time to Be Born Again, Again? (Alma 5)

Occasionally in a Sunday School class, the topic of being born again comes up, and it invariably does so when we reach the famous discourse recorded in Alma 5. Alma asked, "And now behold, I ask of you, my brethren of the church, have ye spiritually been born of God? Have ye received his image in your countenances? Have ye experienced this mighty change in your hearts?" (Alma 5:14).

With these questions ringing in our ears, the teacher may ask the class members, "Have you been born again?" Each time, I expect the group of faithful Latter-day Saints to shout out with one voice, "Yes!" But instead, there is usually an awkward silence, followed by a long discussion about how being born again is a life-long process—not just one event—and how you can get disqualified by disobedience and so on.

Stephen Robinson provided a great explanation of this dilemma:

Brothers and sisters, do Mormons believe in being saved? If I ask my classes that question with just the right twang in my voice, "Do we believe in being saved?" I can generally get about a third of my students to shake their heads and say, "Oh no, no! Those other guys believe in that." What a tragedy! Brothers and sisters, we believe in being saved. That's why Jesus is called the Savior. What good is it to have a savior if no one is saved? It's like having a lifeguard that won't get out of the chair. "There goes another one down. Try the backstroke! Oh, too bad, he didn't make it." We have a savior who can save us from ourselves, from what we lack, from our imperfections, from the carnal individual within us. . . .

There is no other way. Many of us are trying to save ourselves, holding the Atonement of Jesus Christ at arm's distance and saying, "When I've done it, when I've perfected myself, when I've made myself worthy, then I'll be worthy of the Atonement. Then I will allow him in." We cannot do it. That's like saying, "When I am well, I'll take the medicine. I'll be worthy of it then." That's not how it was designed to work.[1]

Jesus asserted that the rebirth of the Spirit is as real as physical birth; it has a before and an after, just as birth does. Certainly a newborn baby has a lot of growing up to do, but we would never say that because there is still much that needs to occur developmentally, the baby has not yet been completely born. (This would be devastating news to a woman in labor!)

According to Alma, if you have taken the name of Christ upon you, you are saved. You dwell in His promised land and are no longer in the wilderness. You have the right to be enveloped about eternally in the arms of His love long before you ever leave this life. In the Book of Mormon, this theme is reinforced over and over. To hem and haw and say that there is still much to do before we're saved is to deny the grace that has given us the gospel, our testimonies, and the glorious truths we embrace. There is still much to do *because* we are saved, and praise be to God that we needn't wait until the next life to have that joy in our hearts.

What It Means to Be Born Again

Perhaps this misconception (excuse the pun) about the rebirth of the Spirit occurs because we think that if we have been born of God, we won't make any more mistakes, have mixed motives, or be weighed down with weaknesses. King Benjamin's converts saying that "we have no more disposition to do evil, but to do good continually" (Mosiah 5:2) may make us feel that unless we feel like doing right all the time, we haven't been born again. I think we need to take into account that King Benjamin's people felt that emotion right then, as the Spirit was resting on them. Follow-up interviews a few months later might have revealed that a few (meaning all) of them still struggled with temptations and weaknesses.

Though in our hearts we long to be with Jesus, we are still sorely tempted. We will continue to stumble and strive, just as the little baby falls innumerable times in learning to walk. But we will know, with the same determination we see in the face of the toddler, that walking with Jesus is what we were born to do. We will never be satisfied until we are back in the arms of our Savior, and He will never desert us until we have safely arrived in His embrace. That assurance changes everything; it is the rebirth of the Spirit, the hope in Christ. To deny that it has occurred is a kind of false humility and, in a small way, is to deny His matchless grace and power.

But What If the Thrill Is Gone?

Alma understood that a relationship with Christ is like a marriage (notice how many times Christ has called Himself the Bridegroom), requiring a lot of upkeep to stay fresh. He challenged us: "And now behold, I say unto you, my brethren, if ye have experienced a change of heart, and if ye have felt to sing the song of redeeming love, I would ask, can ye feel so now?" (Alma 5:26).

Alma listed many ways that we can put the life back in our relationship with our Savior: repent of our sins, humble ourselves, strip ourselves of pride, get over envy, or even stop making fun of other people. In other words, remember the covenants we have made at baptism and in the temple, and then live them. As we do, the life-changing emotions we felt when we first embraced Jesus as our personal Redeemer will fill our souls again and the song of redeeming love will ring in our lives. Like Isaiah, Alma saw the terrible dangers in the sins of pride, materialism, and even snobbery, and thus urged us to resist the temptation of "setting [our] hearts upon the vain things of this world, upon [our] riches," instead following the voice of the Good Shepherd (Alma 5:53). "A shepherd hath called after you and is still calling after you, but ye will not hearken unto his voice! Behold, I say unto you, that the good shepherd doth call you; yea, and in his own name he doth call you, which is the name of Christ" (Alma 5:37–38).

The Book of Mormon is called a testament of Christ for a reason— there is testimony about Him on almost every page. In addition, the four Gospels are there to renew our faith whenever it falters. Elder Bruce R. McConkie said, "[The Gospels] are the source to which we go to fall in love with the Lord."[2] The sacrament, the temple, and our personal worship place us in a position to hear the voice of the Shepherd calling us home. We can use these to get ourselves within hearing range of that voice and feel that love and grace and healing power flowing back into us, and again sing the song of redeeming love. We may then understand what moved Dostoevsky to say, "If anyone could prove to me that Christ is outside the truth, and if the truth really did exclude Christ, I should prefer to stay with Christ and not with truth."[3]

Twenty-Two Ways to Get the Feeling Back

In December 2002, President Howard W. Hunter gave a talk entitled "The Gift of Christmas" in which he listed things we can do to be more like Christ and develop our personal relationship with Him:

Mend a quarrel. Seek out a forgotten friend. Dismiss suspicion and replace it with trust. Write a letter. Give a soft answer. Encourage youth. Manifest your loyalty in word and deed. Keep a promise. Forgo a grudge. Forgive an enemy. Apologize. Try to understand. Examine your demands on others. Think first of someone else. Be kind. Be gentle. Laugh a little more. Express your gratitude. Welcome a stranger. Gladden the heart of a child. Take pleasure in the beauty and wonder of the earth. Speak your love and then speak it again.

According to the Flesh: The Intimate Atonement (Alma 7)

To my mind, the greatest scripture on Christ's redeeming power is found in one of Alma's sermon to the Nephites. It offers breathtaking insight into the Atonement.

> And he shall go forth, suffering pains and afflictions and temptations of every kind; and this that the word might be fulfilled which saith he will take upon him the pains and the sicknesses of his people. And he will take upon him death, that he may loose the bands of death which bind his people; and he will take upon him their infirmities, that his bowels may be filled with mercy, according to the flesh, that he may know according to the flesh how to succor his people according to their infirmities. Now the Spirit knoweth all things; nevertheless the Son of God suffereth according to the flesh that he might take upon him the sins of his people, that he might blot out their transgressions according to the power of his deliverance; and now behold, this is the testimony which is in me. (Alma 7:11–13)

Let's unpack this dense passage; there are three main points:

First, along with His sacrifice on the cross, in Gethsemane Jesus suffered pains, temptations, afflictions, sicknesses, and infirmities of every kind. Now let's define all of those terms.

- Pains—everything that hurts, physically or emotionally
- Temptations—that aching, wrenching desire to do something wrong, including addictions, perversions, and other wayward behaviors
- Afflictions—genetic disorders, handicaps, mental illness, disabilities, and so on
- Sicknesses—cancer, tumors, hormone deficiencies, arthritis; diseases of the organs, skin, bones, muscles; headaches, chronic pain, and so on
- Infirmities—weaknesses like phobias, paralyzing shyness, compulsive behaviors, aggression, anxiety, pessimism, and so on
- Death—entropy, decay, and decline, no matter how great or how small

Second, Christ did all of this so that His "bowels [would be] filled with mercy"; succor us in our pains, temptations, afflictions, sicknesses, and infirmities; and loose the bands of death that bind us (3 Nephi 17:7).

Bowels in the Biblical usage means "gut." The bowels are the lower intestines or the pit of the stomach—exactly where you feel guilt. While we feel guilt and shame in our guts, Jesus's is filled with mercy—and so bowels are also described as "the seat of pity or kindness; hence, tenderness, compassion."[4] *Succor* has its roots in the Latin *succurrere* ("run to the help of") and it combines *sub* ("from below") and *currere* ("run"). There is a beautiful word choice here, because Christ is often described as "[descending] below all things" (D&C 88:6); He literally placed Himself beneath us to lift us up.

Having His "bowels . . . filled with mercy" means that Christ is 100 percent empathetic with us in everything we suffer (3 Nephi 17:7). It may be distressing to think of Christ being torn by such temptations as lust, perversion, and rage, but these are the kinds of emotions He lived through in the Garden. We needn't hide anything from Him; we cannot shock or disappoint Him. He knows us, for He has been wherever we find ourselves, no matter how repellent. His redemptive grace covers *everything* that is wrong with us.

Third, Jesus already understood all of this in the Spirit, but He chose to suffer "according to the flesh" so that He literally, physically could take our sins upon Himself (Alma 7:12). There was something about this process that makes the power of His deliverance so great that it is able to blot out our transgressions.

The phrase "according to the flesh" is repeated three times in this short passage. It seemed important to Alma that we understand that Jesus Christ suffered these things in His body, heart, and mind. Our bodies are such a powerful part of our existences, and sometimes it's hard to have the right attitude toward this troublesome flesh. (The efforts of the ascetics to deny all bodily passions and subjugate the flesh are a negative testimony of the importance of the body.) Christ doesn't hate the body; He embraced incarnation in the flesh and chose to suffer everything that humankind suffers in the flesh. This gave Him a power of deliverance that not only overcomes death but also enables Him to literally "blot out" our mistakes. Imagine how surprising it will be to approach Him at Judgment and find that those sins of which we repented no longer exist. He has the power to forget our sins.

Death Is Conquered; Mankind Is Free

Christ's victory over death seems connected to all of the other victories: over sickness, weakness, and sin. I don't know which comes first, but it is all connected somehow. When Isaiah promised that the lion shall lie down with the lamb, he may have been talking about actual beasts, but I see a soul at peace. Finally, the carnal man and the spiritual man as one man—the fierce, selfish, sinful side tamed and calm, coexisting peacefully with the warm, affectionate, righteous side. There is nothing to fear, nothing to be ashamed of, and nothing to hide. Finally, we will be whole, healed, and home.

We cannot know what it cost the Lord (and His Father) to work out this Atonement for us. One poet imagined Him in the Garden at the crucial moment where He begged the cup to pass, and then accepted it.

> Death's grip seized him.
> He wept. His spirit broke.
> Sweat turned blood. He shook.
> His mouth formed words of pain and spoke.
> "Father, if it's possible, let this hour
> Pass me by."
> A bolt of lightning cut the night!
> In that light
> Swam the cross, its martyr-symbols bright.
> Hands by millions he saw reaching,
> Hands large and small from near and far beseeching,
> And hovering spark-like over the crown of thorn
> The souls of millions yet unborn.
> The murk slunk back into the ground,
> While the dead in their graves their voices found.
> In love's fulness Christ raised himself on high.
> "Father," he cried, "not my
> Will but yours be done."[5]

Though we can never understand what it cost the Lord to suffer for us, we know He did it gladly. It is a small sacrilege to obsess over our faults and weaknesses, to judge and berate ourselves over every mistake—these debts have been paid; Christ took these upon Himself, and He will help us work through them. We do not need to wait until we are well to call upon the Master Physician; instead, we must work with Him to establish a "wellness program" that will help us navigate our responsibilities and relationships in a Christlike way. It's not about us after all; it's all about Him.

To Me He Doth Not Stink: Marital Love in the Scriptures (Alma 19 and 1 Nephi 5)

We aren't given many examples of married love in the Book of Mormon, but there are two I find helpful. Lehi is the only Book of Mormon prophet whose wife is also a character in the narrative. At a moment of great stress, when it appeared that their sons had died as a result of Lehi's obsession with obtaining the records of the Jews, Sariah turned on him. Nephi wrote that she "complained against my father, telling him that he was a visionary man; saying: Behold thou hast led us forth from the land of our inheritance, and my sons are no more, and we perish in the wilderness" (1 Nephi 5:2).

There's a lot of information in this passage—an emotional separation has occurred, shown by the pronouns used: "*you* led us into the wilderness, *my* sons are no more, and, as a result, *we* all are going to die." Think about Sariah's experience and how her expectations have been overturned. Her husband has gone from being a wealthy, respected merchant to a visionary man obsessed with getting some records and taking the whole family into the wilderness, leaving behind everything she has ever known. They had nothing, and she feared her sons were dead. I'm surprised we didn't read about her complaining sooner!

Agree with Thy Adversary Quickly

There are many ways Lehi could have responded to this tirade, but what he did say is rather surprising. Instead of defending himself, he sympathized with his wife. She used the term *visionary* to describe him, and it doesn't sound like a compliment. By repeating the term, he validated her feelings. "I know that I am a visionary man" (1 Nephi 5:4). But then he went on to explain his motivations, and he took the responsibility on himself for the consequences. His pronouns gently reminded her that these were also his sons, and he loved them just as much as she did. "I know that I am a visionary man; for if I had not seen the things of God in a vision I should not have known the goodness of God, but had tarried at Jerusalem, and had perished with my brethren. But behold, I have obtained a land of promise, in the which things I do rejoice; yea, and I know that the Lord will deliver my sons out of the hands of Laban, and bring them down again unto us in the wilderness" (1 Nephi 5:4–5).

Nephi went on to describe the tone of this conversation: "And after this manner of language did my father, Lehi, comfort my mother, Sariah" (1 Nephi 5:6). Instead of making a fight, he quickly agreed with her and comforted her.

There's a lesson here about staying on the same side. When couples square off and oppose each other, little can be accomplished. Even when we are divided on an issue, we can still be united as a couple by how we talk to each other. By acknowledging her frustrations and pains, Lehi validated her feelings. Then, by explaining why he had to do as he was doing, he helped her validate him. Together, they could then move forward.

So how does this translate into our lives? Let's say it's time for prom and your daughter wants to go, but she isn't quite sixteen. You feel that she ought to be able to go, but your spouse opposes it because you have adopted a standard that says she may not date until she is sixteen. You think he or she is silly and too concerned with the letter of the law. Your spouse think it's important to have a standard and stick to it, and that this is a good way to teach her integrity.

Let's think of how Lehi would've approach this. He might say, "I understand that you are excited for Hannah to have this fun experience, and you have raised her to be a wonderful girl we can trust. And I understand that I am often rigid and controlling about the rules and may be too strict at times. But I feel strongly about this issue; I feel that this is what the Lord would have us do." Now your spouse's feelings have been validated and motivations explained, and the Lord has been brought into the conversation.

Once the Lord is involved, we can always pray and ask Him what He thinks about it, and Hannah could also be invited to pray about it.

We don't have to oppose each other just because we don't always agree. We need to stay on the same side.

To Me, You Do Not Stink!

There is a sweet, almost comic moment in the Book of Alma that follows the miraculous conversion of King Lamoni that teaches another important lesson about marital love. After Ammon preached the gospel to him, the king was so overcome that he fell into a comatose state. He was carried to his bed, where he lay for two days, while his family and servants mourned over him. At that point, they prepared to put him in a sepulcher, but his wife didn't really believe that he was dead. She sent for Ammon and said, "I would that ye should go in and see my husband, for he has been laid upon his bed for the space of two days and two nights; and some say that he is not dead, but others say that he is dead and that he stinketh, and that he ought to be placed in the sepulchre; but as for myself, to me he doth not stink" (Alma 19:5).

There is something incredibly touching to me about this moment. When you marry, you give yourself to your spouse, body and soul, and you are commanded to "cleave" to him or her (D&C 42:22). The affection you and your spouse offer each other, both physical and emotional, is life giving. No matter what you face in the outside world, you should know that when you go home, there is one person to whom you are just wonderful. You might be tired and stained by the day's experiences, but to your sweetheart, you are always welcome and loved. You don't stink! I'm always dismayed by married couples who make fun of each other. Teasing and insulting language may get a laugh, but it's not worth the pain it can cause. We know a lot about Lamoni's queen when she said simply, "to me he doth not stink" (Alma 19:5).

Marriage: A Celebration of the Unexpected

Having now been married nearly four decades and having observed many couples around me, I find it interesting how often marriage surprises us. It simply isn't like you expect it to be. How we handle the unexpected can often be the making or undoing of our marital relationships.

In both of these scriptural examples, a couple was married and lived together with one set of expectations, and then there was a dramatic change. This raises the question: What do you do when the person you married turns out to be different than you expected? If you are like most married people, you probably spend a lot of time thinking about what it's like to be married to your spouse. We all do, and we may complain to our family members, friends, or even the Lord about it. Yet how often do you ask yourself, "What it is like to be married to *me*?" Really, what is it like? If you really want to know, God will show you, and it may surprise you. In some ways, being married to you is absolutely wonderful—in other ways, it's probably quite difficult. There might be some fairly simple things you could do to make marriage easier for your spouse without changing your whole nature.

For example, if you're a woman you probably require lots of nurturing and affection, and when you don't get it, you get more needy and more emotional. Most men hate this kind of emotional interchange, and they tend to get more stony and silent the more you rail at them. With God's help, you might be able to see, just for a moment, how all that looks through your husband's eyes. God can help you figure out a way to ask for what you need in a less emotional, more diplomatic way, and then to be satisfied with a little less than you had in mind. You'll be reminded by the Spirit how much this man loves you, even if he doesn't show it the way you want. God can help you see him as he is and yourself as you are. Your husband may not write you poems or sing you love songs, but he loves you. With God's help, you can see the good in him. To you, he will not stink.

As a husband, you may be frustrated by your wife's "nagging" or emotional outbursts. With God's help, you might, for a moment, be able to see life through her eyes and see her worry for every detail of the kid's lives and your well-being. You might see her dependence on you and her fear of the unknown enemies that threaten the home. You might see how much she gives to others every day and how she looks to you for validation and support. And like King Lamoni, you'll be filled with a vision of how great the love of a wife and mother can be—a love that is related to the mother of the Son of God. You might even be filled with a desire to take her by the hand and say (in your own, less flowery way), "Blessed art thou." One great woman I know said to her husband, "I am like a plant, and you are the water. I just need a little water from you every day, or I'll wither and die." He was able to see how his affection could literally sustain her in all that she had to face, and it seemed easier to give her that affection. God can really help us with all of this.

Compassion + Affection = Happiness in Marriage

These two principles of compassion and affection are what keep good marriages alive. When your spouse is angry or frustrated, rather than react with defensiveness, try to understand what she is feeling and have compassion. When your spouse makes a mistake or is under stress, try not to join the world in telling him how he stinks—be the one who continues to see the good in him. And when the unexpected happens, be true to the divine nature within you and see the divine nature within your spouse. Say often that you have faith in her, or that you see great things in him. Be the cheering section, not the peanut gallery.

The Holy Ghost is the greatest marriage counselor in the world. Through the Spirit, we see things as they really are. That means when you invite the Spirit into your marriage, you are going to learn things about yourself that you don't like, but you are also going to feel the Comforter at the same time, letting you know what steps you can take to heal the wounds you may have inflicted on each other. The Spirit can teach you to feel compassion for your frustrated, weary wife, just as Lehi felt for Sariah. And it can fill you with life-giving love that caused the queen to see in Lamoni what no one else could see and help bring her husband back to life. That kind of love is the gift that married people can give each other, when touched by the grace of Christ.

Nourish the Word: When in Doubt, How to Get Out (Alma 32)

When Alma the Younger and his brethren split up and began to work to strengthen the various "stakes" in their faith, they encountered two kinds of unbelievers. First, Alma met Korihor, one of three labeled anti-Christs in the Book of Mormon. Korihor's arguments were the classic existentialist fare: We can't know anything for sure; man is mortal and will die and that is all we can know. The manifestations of the Spirit are the "effect of a frenzied mind" (Alma 30:16), combined with false traditions that were handed down from past generations, and thus they cannot be trusted. There can be no Atonement and every man "fared in this life according to the management of the creature" (Alma 30:17).

Alma's only response to these elaborate arguments was to testify that he knew there was a God. Then he showed God's power after Korihor repeatedly asked for it! Korihor's confession is revealing. After being struck dumb, he wrote that the devil appeared to him as an angel and taught him what to say. But here's the interesting bit: "And I have taught his words; and I taught them because they were pleasing unto the carnal mind; and I taught them, even until I had much success, insomuch that I verily believed that they were true" (Alma 30:53).

With Korihor's arguments in mind, we head to Alma's next adventure—a visit to the Zoramites. These folks had something called a Rameumptom, a stand that held one person at a time. Upon this tower, the designated "pray-er" stood and thanked God for the truth, for their special election to God's grace, and for the fact that they knew there would be no Christ. Mormon tells us that Alma and his brethren were astonished by this strange worship. After a little "district meeting," where Alma blessed everybody and got them all excited about the challenge, they split up and began preaching. And, as is the case in many missions, the poor listened to their message.

It's in this context that Alma preached his great sermon about faith; in it, he answered both the nonbeliever, like Korihor, and the mistaken believer, who was worshipping incorrectly. His answer to all of it was to plant the seed of faith in our hearts, and then to nourish it until it grows into a tree of life.

What's in a Seed?

A seed, according to the website Encyclopedia.com, "is a mature ovule, comprising an embryo or miniature plant along with food reserves, all within a protective seed coat."[6] In human conception terms, a seed is an embryo and its placenta wrapped into one. So what is the seed of faith? We might say it consists of the one or two things we believe—or just wish to believe—wrapped in the ideas and beliefs that will strengthen and nourish that one true idea. *True* is the operative word here because, according to Alma, if we have faith in things that aren't true, they won't grow any more than a dead seed will sprout.

So let's see how this might work in real life. Say you believe in God. You've had a few experiences where you think that something spoke in your heart or mind. If you've been raised in the LDS faith, you connect these experiences to the Church and so believe that the Church is "true"—or in other words, God's authorized organization on earth. And, by extension, that means Joseph Smith was a prophet and the Book of Mormon is God's word, just as is the Bible. And there you have a testimony.

But what is the foundation of that testimony? It may be a few nebulous moments in your life when you felt something beyond yourself. Or it may be a logical construction built upon the fact that the Church system has worked well for your family or for you. Or it may be moments of certainty you have had while reading your scriptures or praying. Whatever the case, at some point—unless you're quite exceptional—you will suddenly begin to doubt all of it. Like a house of cards, when one of the foundation pillars of your testimony falters, the whole thing can come crashing down. What do you do then?

Is Doubt a Good Thing?

Philosophers and theologians differ on whether doubt is a good thing. Søren Kirkegaard said, "Every mental act is composed of doubt and belief, but it is belief that is the positive, it is belief that sustains thought and holds the world together."[7] In other words, doubters don't have a positive impact on the world; believers do. Shakespeare chimed in with a similar sentiment: "Our doubts are traitors, and make us lose the good we oft might win, by fearing to attempt."[8]

These two statements assert that if you doubt, you're doing damage to your beliefs and you aren't really going anywhere; you are paralyzed and thus unable to act. (Think of poor Hamlet.)

But others disagree and, in fact, see doubts as important components to faith. Paul Tillich said, "Doubt isn't the opposite of faith; it is an element of faith."[9] And the great Buddha himself encouraged us, "Doubt everything. Find your own light."[10]

So what is the answer here? Is doubt a good or bad thing? I think the answer is yes—it's a good thing and a bad thing. Doubt can destroy a testimony or be the beginning of an unshakeable one. The symbol of the seed helps us understand how this works.

Die to Live

To germinate, a seed must break open and die. Jesus said, "Verily, verily, I say unto you, Except a corn of wheat fall into the ground and die, it abideth alone: but if it die, it bringeth forth much fruit" (John 12:24).

It can be a painful thing when the beliefs we've held since childhood are challenged and even cracked open. This can be a time when the seed dies or when it really begins to live. The difference between life and death for the testimony is how we choose to nourish that seed when those cracks of doubt occur.

Alma said that faith can begin with nothing more than a "desire to believe" (Alma 32:27). This, at first, seems self-contradictory. How can we prove something empirically if we start by wanting it to be true? A fascinating wiki called "Feast Upon the Word" explains the conundrum this way:

> It is significant that this is a desire *to believe* instead of a desire to know the truth. This minimum case begins with a desire that the gospel is true—we have to start by wanting it to be so. The *experiment* Alma teaches us then, is no impartial experiment. Those for whom truth means only those things we can discover through impartial analysis, will find no way here to discover these truths. In their eyes Alma begins the experiment by stacking the deck in his favor because the experiment only begins with those who want to believe that the gospel

is true. We see here that God has set up this world up in such a way that the most important truths, [for example] God is a merciful god who wants to hear from all his children, rather than hearing only once a week, in a synagogue from the well-off, are revealed only to those who, at a minimum, want to believe in such. And, as we see in the surrounding chapters, those who want instead to believe in a God who elected just themselves to be holy "whilst all around [them] are elected to be cast by [God's] wrath down to hell," to such people, so long as their desires remain so, Alma has no way to give them faith.[11]

Korihor called the desire to believe the "effect of a frenzied mind" (Alma 30:16), and certainly any thoughtful person questions his or her conclusions when they're colored by the desire that they be true. But God's science appears to have different rules than people's; in God's definition of knowledge, desire is tantamount. You have to *want* the gospel to be true and for Jesus to be the Savior; you have to be emotionally invested in the truth before it will be manifest to you. Alma isn't worried by this because a principle that isn't true will not germinate; it won't grow and produce what he called "swelling motions" (Alma 32:28) that let you know what you are wanting to believe is something that is real and true. Thus, the Zoramites on their Rameumptom could recite a prayer filled with falsehoods, but it had no power to move or change their hearts. They wanted to believe it, but it was a dead thing, not an embryo filled with life, waiting to burst out.

What to Do with Doubt

Today, we often hear that people are quick to believe their doubts and doubt their beliefs. Once again, I worry when we make people feel bad for doubting. Many young members have encountered speculations on the Internet about the Prophet Joseph Smith or multiple accounts of the First Vision or other revelations about the early leaders of the Church that are different from the idealized portraits with which they were raised. Suddenly, doubt has cracked their seeds of faith—in many cases, they feel that if they have such doubts, it must mean that they don't believe. Another fact about seeds is interesting: "Seeds often exhibit dormancy, meaning they fail to germinate even when provided with adequate water and suitable temperature conditions. Dormancy acts to prevent germination until conditions are right. This dormancy may be broken by proper exposure to light or darkness."[12]

Notice that seeds can be jarred into germination by either light or darkness. We can grow through those times when we're inspired and filled with certainty and also through those times when our beliefs are dashed upon the rocks of doubt. Doubting doesn't mean you don't believe; it means that your seed is cracking open, ready to grow. But that seed will die if, at this crucial moment, you don't give it nourishment.

The Care and Feeding of Faith

What do we feed the seed to cause it to germinate? Alma said that it consists of "looking forward with an eye of faith" (Alma 32:40). And then he went on for the next few chapters teaching people to pray, to converse with God, and to involve Him in all their daily dilemmas. He encouraged them to understand true doctrine about Christ and His Atonement. He rehearsed the law of Moses and taught them how it pointed to Christ. He talked to them about soft hearts, continual repentance, humility, and complete reliance upon Christ. In other words, he encouraged them to concentrate on living the things they knew were true.

If it's wrong to doubt, I'm in big trouble because that is the kind of person I am. I am encouraged that Jesus was so accepting of His Apostle Thomas. The Lord patiently said to him, "Be not faithless, but believing" (John 20:28). As a born doubter, I have learned to embrace my doubts as a part of my journey of faith. But I don't allow them to determine my destiny. That is determined by my beliefs, and my beliefs are based in Alma's definition of what is real. "O then, is not this real? I say unto you, Yea, because it is light; and whatsoever is light, is good, because it is discernible, therefore ye must know that it is good" (Alma 32:35).

Things may be factual and not be real. You may learn unsettling things about Joseph Smith or the Book of Mormon—and they may even be factual. But what is real about Joseph Smith and the Book of Mormon is that they both ooze with light. There is so much inspiration, joy, love, and Christianity in the Book of Mormon and in the teachings of the Prophet Joseph Smith that it is overwhelming. Just Alma 32 alone is a marvelous work and a wonder! To miss the treasure in the field, to bypass the rich vein of gold because it is surrounded by crude granite, is to miss something precious for the sake of a few facts.

Ask the hard questions. You don't have to live a lie. If you can't get satisfactory answers to all of them, keep thinking, praying, and doubting certain things! But nourish the seed—don't let it die. Live the truths you've been given; and because this really is a good seed, your life will be filled with discernible light and real joy. And here we are, back at Lehi's glorious tree of life, only what a surprise awaits— the tree is each one of us, a glorious receptacle of God's own life:

> And because of your diligence and your faith and your patience with the word in nourishing it, that it may take root in you, behold, by and by ye shall pluck the fruit thereof, which is most precious, which is sweet above all that is sweet, and which is white above all that is white, yea, and pure above all that is pure; and ye shall feast upon this fruit even until ye are filled, that ye hunger not, neither shall ye thirst. Then, my brethren, ye shall reap the rewards of your faith, and your diligence, and patience, and long-suffering, waiting for the tree to bring forth fruit unto you. (Alma 32:42–43)

An Acrostic on Faith

Alma 32:28 uses an acrostic, or a composition of words in which certain letters in each line form a word or words. In the English translation, Alma was speaking about a seed, and then spells out "seed" by using the verbs *swell, enlarge, enlighten,* and *delicious.* There is no way to know, of course, whether the acrostic was present in the original, though there are some examples of acrostic poetry in the Psalms.

Spiritual Geriatrics: The Resurrection and the Second Law of Thermodynamics (Alma 40–42)

I don't really know anything about physics, but I'm interested in the second law of thermodynamics because I once heard Hugh Nibley connect it to resurrection. I've thought of the two as related principles ever since.

The first law of thermodynamics asserts that there's a finite amount of matter in the universe, an amount that has been there since its inception. Matter can be changed into various forms, but it never ceases to exist. The second law of thermodynamics says that this matter is in a continual state of entropy—that is, of moving from a state of usability (for progress, growth and repair) to an unusable state. The logical conclusion of this entropic process is the eventual death of the universe.[13]

Resurrection and Restoration—Entropy in Reverse

The overthrow of the traditional biblical view of the Creation during the eighteenth and nineteenth centuries seemed to fix an unbridgeable gulf between science and faith. If God created the world, then it must have had a beginning point, and because the science of that day did not support that idea, the biblical Creation narrative was flatly rejected. More recent discoveries that the universe did have a beginning suggest that there may be a place for God in a scientific view of the universe. Stephen Hawking wrote, "In an unchanging universe a beginning in time has to be imposed by some being outside the universe; there is no physical necessity for a beginning. On the other hand, if the universe is expanding, there may be physical reasons why there had to be a beginning. God could have created the universe at any time in the past."[14]

Obviously, this tectonic shift in the foundations of modern science hasn't been met with joy by many. Robert Jastrow, a NASA astronomer, wrote that many of his fellow astronomers were as dismayed by the idea that there might be a creative force guiding the universe as theologians were by the scientific explanation of the Creation. "For the scientist who has lived by his faith in the power of reason, the story ends like a bad dream. He has scaled the mountains of ignorance; he is about to conquer the highest peak; as he pulls himself over the final rock, he is greeted by a band of theologians who have been sitting there for centuries."[15]

If the universe had a beginning and is continually expanding and using up a finite amount of energy, then the universe will one day come to an end. However, scriptures teach us that, in fact, this process will be reversed through Christ's Resurrection.

Alpha and Omega, the Beginning and the End

In a letter to his son, Alma described the progress of mankind—not in a linear fashion, but more like a sphere of existence that has, at its center point, the Atonement and Resurrection of Jesus Christ. It doesn't matter, he told Corianton, when the various stages of the resurrection occur, because "all is as one day with God, and time only is measured unto men" (Alma 40:8).

Thus the Atonement isn't just the most important event in history: history actually begins with the Atonement. This is how the Lord's redeeming power was efficacious long before the actual events occurred. Jesus was called "the lamb slain from the foundation of the world" (Revelation 13:8). King Benjamin declared, "Salvation was, and is, and is to come, in and through the atoning blood of Christ" (Mosiah 3:18). It's one eternal round, with Christ at its center. Time is only measured by people.

Christ's Resurrection, according to Alma, exerts a power on the universe that "bringeth about the restoration of those things of which has been spoken by the mouths of the prophets" (Alma 40:22). Entropy, or the gradual decline of matter through the expenditure of energy, is reversed by the power of the Atonement and the Resurrection. The earth itself will "be renewed and receive its paradisiacal glory" (Articles of Faith 1:10). All human beings will rise at some point, and "the soul shall be restored to the body, and the body to the soul" (Alma 40:23).

With the discoveries of the Hubble Space Telescope, scientists were forced to accept the fact that the universe had a beginning and perhaps even a guiding force. At some point, scientific theory will again have to be amended to accept a reversal of the second law of thermodynamics. Entropy is not eternal—life is.

What Does the Resurrection Mean to Me Right Now?

Certainly our knowledge of resurrection is precious to us because all of us suffer the loss of loved ones, and each of us must eventually suffer death ourselves. "The sting of death is swallowed up in Christ" (Mosiah 16:8). But beyond that, an understanding of the power of Christ's Resurrection can serve as a key to a more abundant life right now.

Jesus continually used the words *light* and *life* in connection with Himself. "I am the light of the world" (John 8:12). And, "I am come that they might have life, and . . . have it more abundantly" (John 10:10). As we invite the Savior into our daily lives through worship, meditation, and concerted attempts to follow His guidance, we actually grow more alive. The power of resurrection can filter down into our daily lives and infuse us with a more abundant life. Brigham Young described a process that reverses entropy: "The elements that every individual is made of and lives in possess the Godhead. . . . The Deity within us is the great principle that causes us to increase, and to grow in grace and truth. . . . Commence with it, go through the vail into eternity with it, and still continue, and the end thereof no man on earth knoweth, nor the angels in heaven."[16]

Parley P. Pratt described the enlivening influence of the Spirit in our lives:

> The gift of the Holy Ghost . . . quickens all the intellectual faculties, increases, enlarges, expands and purifies all the natural passions and affections; and adapts them, by the gift of wisdom, to their lawful use. It inspires, develops, cultivates and matures all the fine-toned sympathies, joys, tastes, kindred feelings, and affections of our nature. It inspires virtue, kindness, goodness, tenderness, gentleness, and charity. It develops beauty of person, form and features. It tends to health, vigor, animation, and social feeling. It invigorates all the faculties of the physical and intellectual man. It strengthens, and gives tone to the nerves. In short, it is, as it were, marrow to the bone, joy to the heart, light to the eyes, music to the ears, and life to the whole being.[17]

This view is far different than viewing ourselves as beings in a state of gradual decline. If you're living in Christ's grace, you aren't in a state of entropy, but rather in a state of eternal progression. Though your body may grow weak and die, your essence, your spirit only grows brighter and stronger. Eventually, that spirit will be restored to your body and you will go forward on an eternal adventure of discovery and joy.

Are You a Spiritual Geriatric?

Several years ago, my husband, Craig, was standing in a grocery store line with a friend. In front of them stood an old, grumpy man who was angry about the length of the wait. When his turn finally came, he really let the poor checker have a piece of his mind. As they left the store, Craig turned to his friend and said, "How do we keep from becoming that guy?" They had a long discussion about how easy it is to grow angry and cynical when getting older. We've laughed about that many times, now that we're suffering some of the aches and pains that inevitably go with aging. As President Hinckley once wryly observed, "The so-called golden years are laced with lead."[18]

Growing older is extremely challenging, not just physically but also spiritually. The vicissitudes of life can wear away our optimism and sense of fun and adventure. It's easy to turn into a negative, complaining, old person. This is a kind of spiritual entropy; it is as if our spiritual energy got used up and there is no more to replace it. That is what the power of the resurrection can reverse. The Holy Spirit can regenerate our tired, cranky spirits and fill us with a newness of life, enabling us to see the best in others and fully enjoy the beautiful world around us. Though there is suffering and disappointment in life, there is also a hope in Christ that can sustain us. And we can always be on the Lord's errand, even if our capacities are limited. We can always radiate His love to others.

If you're feeling a bit like a spiritual geriatric, take a stroll through the scriptures and read everything in there about light, life, and resurrection. It will be like a drink from the fountain of youth. Now that's what I call thermodynamics!

There Really Is a Plan

One of the most important doctrines in the Book of Mormon is that the Lord has a plan of salvation and that the plan has a framework that helps people understand why they are on earth and where they will go after. The plan of salvation—known by many names in the Book of Mormon—is mentioned approximately thirty times in the book. Elder Merrill J. Bateman said, "The word 'plan' as it relates to the Plan of Salvation does not appear in the King James Bible. There is no mention of a plan, and no phrase resembling the Plan of Salvation appears in any biblical translation."[19]

The Stripling Warriors: Motherhood Is Not for Sissies (Alma 56)

The story of the stripling warriors is a story about overcoming fear. These two thousand young men faced overwhelming odds in battle, yet they entered into it without the fear that paralyzes most people faced with such horror.

Helaman described the moment when he offered them the chance to retreat, but, as one, they chose to go forward: "Now they never had fought, yet they did not fear death; and they did think more upon the liberty of their fathers than they did upon their lives; yea, they had been taught by their mothers, that if they did not doubt, God would deliver them. And they rehearsed unto me the words of their mothers, saying: We do not doubt our mothers knew it" (Alma 56:48–49).

We might ask ourselves the question, How do you become the kind of mother who raises fearless, faith-filled children?

Motherhood Is Scary

Mothers know all about fear because motherhood is the scariest job in the world. And it's not just sending kids off to war that mothers have to fear—mothers are afraid of traffic, illness, gangs, bad influences, bullies, and boogeymen. They fear anything that could be a potential threat to their children, from a speck on the floor that could be choked on to a speck on the horizon that could grow into a storm that makes the roads unsafe. We put on brave faces for the kids, but we lie awake at night worrying about everything that could possibly go wrong for our children.

The Book of Mormon offers some comfort, telling us how to overcome at least some of the fear mothers suffer. Mormon said, "I fear not what man can do; for perfect love casteth out all fear" (Moroni 8:16). He seems to be saying that to have less fear in our lives, we need to have more love. This seems counterintuitive in a way, because isn't it our love for our children that's causing us to worry and fear for them? He must have been talking about a different kind of love.

The important qualifier here is "perfect" love. This means the kind of love that God has for us. His love for us is similar to our love for our children in its fierce devotion and willingness to protect us at any cost. (Jesus actually described Himself as a mother hen, gathering her chicks under her wing—a motherly image if there ever was one.) Where God's love differs from ours is in its disinterestedness. God loves us without any selfish element involving His own satisfaction. Our lives matter to God, not because they help define Him, but rather simply *because* they matter to Him. Taking that self-centered element out of our love for our children is something God can help us with. And that will also help cast out fear.

How Perfect Love Casts Out Fear

This doesn't mean that we stop suffering when evil, sickness, and sadness befall our kids. We will always do that, as God does. Remember how He wept as He showed Enoch a vision of His children? When Enoch wondered how God, who is all-powerful, could weep, God responded simply, "Should not the heavens weep, seeing these shall suffer?" (Moses 7:37). Though suffering is always part and parcel of parenthood, our lives don't have to be governed by fear and worry if we learn to love our children as God does. When we stop fearing what people can do, we know our children are in God's hands—come what may. The covenants that seal us in the temple offer powerful promises about the power of God in the lives of our posterity; we can get up every day and send our children out into the world knowing that, whatever happens, their lives—and ours—are part of a larger plan.

Many years ago, a dear friend had a child die in the womb the very week it was due. It was a terrible heartache, of course; the loss of a child is our worst fear. Later, she shared with me a sacred moment that came to her just a few days before this happened. She was taking a bath (one of those rare moments of peace and quiet a mother has), and the Spirit spoke these words in her mind: *If you lost this child, you could stand it.* That was all, but it was enough. When the unspeakable sorrow of losing that baby came to her some days later, she knew she wasn't alone. And she knew that no matter how great the grief, with Christ's help she could stand it. Sometimes, that's all we've got.

It's about Them, Not Us

A second (and equally important, I think) way that perfect love casts out fear is in relation to how our children impact our own lives. Let's be honest, much of who we are and what we think of ourselves is bound up in our children. Our kids are raised to reflect our values, traditions, and beliefs, and when they go contrary to those, it's natural to feel some anger and resentment. This can lead to serious rifts—sometimes permanent damage—in the fabric of the family. Nearly every parent has said of a child, at one time or other, "How could she (or he) do this to me?" Whether at age two, twelve, or twenty-two, it can feel like our children's actions are specifically designed to hurt us when, in reality, they're just trying to figure out their own lives.

As we incorporate the principle of Christlike love into our mothering, we may find that there's far more selfishness in us than we'd ever dreamed. If our love fails us when our children turn on us, we must fearlessly face that part of ourselves that wants a child to make us look like a "successful" parent. We cannot read enough self-help books or get enough therapy to overcome this spiritual malady; the cure must come from God. Moroni said that the only way to get love that doesn't fail is to "pray . . . with all the energy of heart, that ye may be filled with [Christ's] love" (Moroni 7:48).

Simply asking every day for Christ to help us love a child as He does can be a revelatory experience. Eventually, the anger, embarrassment, and resentment fade, and we are able to see that child as a precious son or daughter of God, on a path that is different than we anticipated but still under Christ's protective grace.

Somehow we stop worrying what people will think of us when they see that tantrum, tattoo, or attitude and can concentrate on the child. We no longer fear what anyone, including our own children, can do to us because we are out of the equation. Heavenly Father is a Being of joy and light, though many of His children cause Him pain and suffering. It would be hard to imagine God fearing anyone or anything. Overcoming the fear of how our children's behavior will impact our own lives is a key to peace and joy, even in a family divided by differing beliefs and behaviors.

Mothering Never Ends

One of the greatest lessons on mothering, for me, came from a wonderful grandmother when my kids were still all at home. I was complaining about one of our kids, who was worrying me in some way, and Norma said, "Hey, you think you have problems now? Just wait until they all start getting divorced!" She then told me about a son who was going through a divorce and how helpless she felt as she witnessed his poor decisions.

Norma was right. As you grow older, you continue to suffer with your children. But, though you may not be able to control their lives, you can still influence them in a Christlike way. This must become our focus as our children grow older.

My wonderful mother is a great example to me of how to navigate the tricky waters of parenting adult children. Several years ago, we had a wedding in our family that was a bittersweet one.

While we were thrilled that my niece was being married in the temple, we were sad because a divided family would gather for this wedding and my brother wouldn't be in the temple to see his daughter married.

For my mother, this represented an almost unbearable heartache. As a grandmother, she wanted to be there for her granddaughter, but as a mother she could hardly bear to go into the temple and leave her son (a wonderful man and an outstanding father) sitting outside. She wondered if, rather than attending the ceremony, she'd be better off waiting with him.

When Mom and I talked about her dilemma, I suggested that maybe she use her advanced age as an excuse and just decide to be sick that morning and only show up for the reception. She liked that idea and even considered just "recusing" herself from the whole event. A few days later, however, she told me that as she was sitting and thinking about that sad situation, the Spirit spoke in her heart: *You've done a lot of hard things, Jeanie, and you can do this too, because I'll help you.* And He did. She was able to extend love and support to everyone involved; in the end it was a beautiful day. She knew where to be and when to be there. As mothers, we are often torn with the need to be several places at once. We can't do that, but the Savior can, and He can guide us through the particulars.

Motherhood Isn't for Sissies—It's for Saints

The *LDS Mother's Almanac* tells it like it is: "Real mothers, contrary to most Sunday School tributes, are not always heroic and strong. Real mothers are not perfect examples of human virtue. Real mothers burn the toast, lose their patience, and fail to meet their children's needs. Real mothers sometimes lose their marbles and their minds. Real mothers sometimes feel overwhelmed and discouraged. No matter how imperfect you may be, however, you can still choose to love."[20]

One emotion every mother understands is fear—another is the worry that whatever you are doing isn't quite enough. The only powers strong enough to defeat fear and worry are faith, hope, and love. Christ has experienced and taken upon Himself every fear; He can fill in the gaps where we fail in our efforts, and He can teach us to love as He does. What you're doing as a mother right now is enough because Christ is mighty to save. And as we turn our children toward Him, we connect them to a foundation upon which, if they build, they will never fall (see Helaman 5:12).

The nurturing of children, at any age, is the work of God, and bringing souls to Christ is the most important work in the world. The great mothers profiled in Helaman's letter challenge us take a second look at where we're spending our time and energy and see if we can infuse a little more spiritual power into our mothering, with the help of faith, hope, and charity. Before they could teach their children not to fear, we know that those mothers had to overcome their own fears and worries through their commitments to Christ. Someday, with God's help, our children will say of us, "We do not doubt our mothers knew it" (Alma 56:48).

Notes

1. Stephen E. Robinson, "Believing Christ: A Practical Approach to the Atonement," *BYU Speeches*, May 29, 1990.

2. Bruce R. McConkie, "Drink from the Fountain," *Liahona*, December 1985.

3. Fyodor Dostoyevsky, "Letter To Mme. N. D. Fonvisin" (1854), as published in *Letters of Fyodor Michailovitch Dostoevsky to his Family and Friends*, translated by Ethel Golburn Mayne, Letter XXI (1914), 71.

4. "Bowels," *The Imperial Dictionary*, edited by John Ogilvie (London: Blackie and Son, 1562), 229.

5. Annette von Droste-Hülshoff, "Gethsemane," *Divine Inspiration: The Life of Jesus in World Poetry*, edited by Robert Atwan, George Dardess, and Peggy Rosenthal (New York: Oxford University Press, 1998), 404.

6. "Seeds," *Encyclopedia*, http://www.encyclopedia.com/topic/Seeds.aspx.

7. Søren Kirkegaard, as quoted in Timothy Keller, *Walking with God through Pain and Suffering* (New York: Dutton, 2014).

8. William Shakespeare, *Measure for Measure*, act one, scene four 1623.

9. Paul Tillich, *Goodreads*, see http://www.goodreads.com/quotes/129557-doubt-isn-t-the-opposite-of-faith-it-is-an-element.

10. Gautama Buddha, *Goodreads*, see http://www.goodreads.com/quotes/119832-doubt-everything-find-your-own-light.

11. "Alma 32:26–43," *Feast Upon the Word*, posted October 31, 2015, http://feastupontheword.org/Alma_32:26-43.

12. "Seeds," *Encyclopedia*, http://www.encyclopedia.com/topic/Seeds.aspx.

13. "Second Law of Thermodynamics," *All About . . .*, http://www.allaboutscience.org/second-law-of-thermodynamics.htm.

14. Stephen Hawking, *A Brief History of Time* (New York: Bantam Books, 1988), 9.

15. Robert Jastrow, *God and the Astronomers* (Reader's Library, Inc., 1992), 116.

16. Brigham Young, *Journal of Discourses*, 26 vols. (London: Latter-day Saints' Book Depot, 1854–86), 1:93.

17. Parley P. Pratt, *Key to the Science of Theology*, ninth edition (Salt Lake City: Deseret Book, 1965), 101.

18. Gordon B. Hinckley, "This Is the Work of the Master," *Ensign*, May 1995.

19. Merrill J. Bateman, as quoted in Marianne Holman Prescott, " 'The coming forth of the Book of Mormon' discussed at BYU symposium," *Deseret News*, October 29, 2015.

20. Janene W. Baasgaard, *The LDS Mother's Almanac* (Salt Lake City: Deseret Book, 2003), 458.

Your Stories and Thoughts

Helaman: Spiritual Wickedness in High Places

The Truth Is Out There: Conspiracy Theories (Helaman 1–2)

The book of Helaman introduces us to a character who transforms the narrative of the Book of Mormon: the crafty, wicked Gadianton. "For there was one Gadianton, who was exceedingly expert in many words, and also in his craft, to carry on the secret work of murder and of robbery; therefore he became the leader of the band of Kishkumen" (Helaman 2:4).

Mormon lets us know that the Gadianton band, with its secret oaths and plans for seizing power, would nearly prove the undoing of the entire civilization: "And behold, in the end of this book ye shall see that this Gadianton did prove the overthrow, yea, almost the entire destruction of the people of Nephi" (Helaman 2:13). So we find that a small group of dedicated criminals step in to take advantage of the natural rivalry between the Nephites and the Lamanites. The animosity between these two peoples made them vulnerable and provided opportunities for this self-serving group to seize control.

Conspiracies are the dark opposite of covenants. God's people bind themselves to Him and each other with sacred covenants, oaths, and ordinances. Evil groups use many of the same methods, only rather than promises of peace and joy, such bind their members together with promises of power and wealth and threats of retaliation in the case of disloyalty—threats so terrifying that the members would keep each others' secrets forever.

What's Really Going On?

History is rife with all sorts of conspiracies, imagined and real: the moon landing was faked. The Bermuda Triangle is real. John F. Kennedy's death was a carefully orchestrated plot. The US government is hiding alien remains at Area 51 in New Mexico. Hitler and Eva Braun escaped from Germany and lived in South America for decades before they died. The Holocaust never really happened. Armenians made up the story of their genocide to infiltrate American cities. Elvis is still alive!

Conspiracy theories seem to grow out of many major historical incidents. The details of these theories may change, but the elements are always consistent: a secret group with a secret plan (about which the average person is blissfully unaware) seeks to obtain power by perpetrating certain acts of deception or violence. The Book of Mormon reminds us that the reason so many of these theories abound is because sometimes conspiracies really do exist and pose a threat. The trick is to understand when we are really being threatened and when we are being deceived.

Americans, with their fierce feelings of independence, seem to be particularly attracted to conspiracy theories. A fascinating study by two university professors noted that Thomas Jefferson and the other Founding Fathers believed that a master plan was at the heart of the oppressive laws held over the colonies. The Declaration of Independence contains a list of twenty-seven accusations made against the king in this regard. Though there was no organized conspiracy (just muddled foreign policy), the American response to it had a happy outcome: our nation. The study continued, "As with many things, where the Founders have led, Americans have followed in droves. A steady stream of conspiracy theories has flowed in the years since the founding, imputing anti-American conspiracies to the British, French,

Spanish, Bavarian Illuminati, Freemasons, Slave Power, Abolitionists, Catholics, Jews, Mormons, Muslims, communists, capitalists, and many, many more. No powerful group has escaped the attention of conspiracy theorists."[1]

Conspiracy theories tend to fall into five main categories:

Enemy from the outside—the belief that people are infiltrating our society to gain control over us. Groups like the John Birch Society (dedicated to combating communist infiltration) address this issue.

Enemy from within—the belief that groups are forming within the society to undermine it. Terrorist sleeper cells are examples of this, as well as the mafia and the Ku Klux Klan. Mormons and Jews are often accused of attempting to gain financial control over certain segments of the economy.

Enemy above—the belief that alien beings, or a few mega-wealthy men, are secretly controlling many of the events in history. Theories about the central bank, the Federal Reserve, and the real cause of most wars are part of this sort of theory.

Enemy below—the belief that groups from the lower classes are banding together to overthrow society. Ethnic, class, and racial prejudices figure largely in this type of theory. Whites fear blacks, factory owners fear unions, Christians fear Jews, and so on.

Benevolent conspiracies—these include groups that are believed to be secretly attempting to improve society by unconventional means. The Skull and Bones group from Yale (from which many world leaders come), the Freemasons, and Opus Dei (an inner circle in the Catholic church) are examples of groups that are suspected of manipulating events with a "benevolent" (nonfinancial) motive.[2]

Is It Real or Is It Paranoia?

From groups that oppose fluoridation of the water to "preppers" hiding out in bomb shelters, conspiracy theories address the notion of control. We don't like to think that others control our lives, and we'd like to feel that we have some control over what happens next to us. The idea that there is a unified power behind terrifying, seemingly random events (such as school shootings or airline disasters) may offer a sense of safety when the world seems to be spinning out of control. (There is even a theory that the Japanese tsunami of 2011 was caused by a carefully placed nuclear bomb detonation in the Pacific Ocean.) Conspiracy theories often sound ridiculous, unless you happen to believe one—then its very incongruity lends to its credence.

Sadly, conspiracy theories often grow out of our own fears and prejudices. History shows that whenever one group feels threatened by another, conspiracy theories sprout up that tend to justify aggressive behavior for "protection." In this way, Hitler's propaganda about the secret plans of the Jews to control their economy caused the German people to abandon their sense of moral rectitude and participate in genocide. Turkish propaganda about Armenians had the same result, as did white supremacist literature in South Africa. There are dozens of conspiracy theories about Mormons, ranging from secret plans to overthrow the American government to hidden caverns and tunnels under Salt Lake City, and these have justified persecution against the Church since its beginning.

How Do We Know What to Believe?

So how do we know which theories are true and which are paranoid fantasies? We may never have all of the facts on these matters, but both the Book of Mormon and our current leaders offer clear guidelines to protect us from being deceived. Here are two things we can count on:

Though conspiracies exist, the Church isn't one of them. God's prophet tells the truth. The prophet isn't hiding some secret knowledge about the coming apocalypse that he isn't telling us. When the danger is real, our prophet speaks up, so we should listen to what he actually says rather than what we think he might be keeping from us. For example, when Gordon B. Hinckley encouraged us to be prepared yet balanced, we should take him at his word:

> I am familiar, as are you, with the declarations of modern revelation that the time will come when the earth will be cleansed and there will be indescribable distress, with weeping and mourning and lamentation. . . . Now, I do not wish to be an alarmist. I do not wish to be a prophet of doom. I am optimistic. I do not believe the time

is here when an all-consuming calamity will overtake us. I earnestly pray that it may not. . . . As we have been continuously counseled for more than 60 years, let us have some food set aside that would sustain us for a time in case of need. But let us not panic nor go to extremes. Let us be prudent in every respect.[3]

The most dangerous conspiracies are spiritual. The scriptures state repeatedly that the greatest dangers we face are not temporal but spiritual. We're encouraged to stay out of debt and gather a supply of food, cash, and essentials in case of emergencies. But beyond that, our leaders continually focus on the spiritual challenges we face, knowing the dangers that may come from natural disasters, wars, or other social upheavals are actually far less damaging from an eternal vantage point. Temporal trials may seem to threaten our lives, but spiritual dangers can steal our souls.

The Gadianton robbers were real; there was a conspiracy to take control of the government and oppress the people. But as the people lived righteously, it was as if they developed spiritual antibodies that made them immune to the cancerous influence of these evil men. This wouldn't have happened if their time had been spent doing meticulous research into every kind of conspiracy that existed. Instead, they studied the scriptures and tried to repent. And as long as they lived the gospel, they were happy and prosperous and were guided away from deception and evil. It wasn't storing enough ammunition to defeat an army that saved them—it was putting on the armor of God.

The Gadianton wars finally ended in the years after Christ's birth, when the Nephites defeated their army, put the surviving robbers in prison, and "did cause the word of God to be preached unto them" (3 Nephi 5:4). They understood that the only way to defeat an enemy is to have the Lord turn him or her into an ally.

Again, President Gordon B. Hinckley summed it up beautifully: "We need to make both temporal and spiritual preparation for the events prophesied at the time of the Second Coming. And the preparation most likely to be neglected is the one less visible and more difficult—the spiritual. A 72-hour kit of temporal supplies may prove valuable for earthly challenges, but, as the foolish virgins learned to their sorrow, a 24-hour kit of spiritual preparation is of greater and more enduring value."[4]

Off the Wall: Samuel the Lamanite Talks to Teens (Helaman 13–15)

I've worked with the youth for much of my time in the Church, and I think that perhaps the most challenging and rewarding calling with teenagers is teaching early-morning seminary. You have to get up pretty early in the morning to fool a group of teenagers, and I love that about them. Teaching early-morning seminary, you soon discover that if you're less than honest with teens, they quickly disappear, and you'll be facing an empty room. High school kids are at the age where the brain kicks in and begins to question everything that has been loaded into it up to that point. This can be challenging for adults, but I find it stimulating as well.

Studies of the teenage brain tell us that during the period between ages thirteen and twenty-five, the brain, already 90 percent formed, enters a period of refinement. Unused synapses are "pruned" and the frontal areas, so crucial for making choices and controlling behavior, become more streamlined and able to function rapidly. Some of the more annoying qualities of adolescence (thrill-seeking, peer-clinging, defiance) are actually essential in preparing the teenage brain for the great "exodus" that will define his or her future—namely, the move away from home and family. A recent article in *National Geographic* made this interesting statement about adolescence: "The period's uniqueness rises from genes and developmental processes that . . . play an amplified role during this key transitional period: producing a creature optimally primed to leave a safe home and move into unfamiliar territory. The move outward from home is the most difficult thing that humans do, as well as the most critical—not just for individuals but for a species that has shown an unmatched ability to master challenging new environments."[5]

Into the Wilderness in Search of a Promised Land

The Book of Mormon chronicles the move from a safe home into unfamiliar territory. Because this also aptly describes the spiritual path of a teenager, they can relate to the various groups wandering into the wilderness in the Book of Mormon. In their strong desire to express their feelings, adolescents can understand it when Samuel the Lamanite stood up on the wall and spoke "the words of the Lord which he doth put into my heart" (Helaman 13:5).

Samuel's message was not a warm, cozy one. With a heavenly perspective, he spoke in a warning voice about the dangers out there, and he was not afraid to tell it like it was. On the other hand, his was also a hopeful, idealogical voice that believed wholeheartedly in the Savior. While most everyone else had turned cynical, Samuel was a true believer and testified of the coming of Jesus. Like Joseph Smith, he was unafraid to raise a warning voice, even when everyone around him responded with hostility. He was a hero. Episodes like the preaching of Samuel the Lamanite are what make the Book of Mormon such great reading for teenagers.

On the Road to Spiritual Maturity

There are many reasons the Book of Mormon is a great primer for teens. For one thing, it's difficult and causes the mind to stretch and reach, which is good for that still-growing muscle in their heads. Better still, most of the great theological questions are raised in the Book of Mormon and answered in thoughtful, inspiring ways. While it is full of wonderful promises about the Savior and His mission, the book is also a tragic saga of what happens to people when they let go of the iron rod and wander off on strange paths—something teenagers often long to do. Prophets like Samuel the Lamanite were not afraid to let people know that if they didn't repent and keep the commandments, then destruction was just around the corner. The same is true today. Accepting the real consequences of our actions is a vital part of growing into spiritual adulthood.

Unfortunately, in today's society, spiritual adults are something of an endangered species, and thus the climate is a pretty chilly one for thinking believers. In school, in the media, and in almost every other setting, our kids are taught that to believe in God is foolish and that intelligent people put aside superstitious nonsense as they reach adulthood. Samuel the Lamanite and other Book of Mormon prophets offer a strong voice in the wilderness, assuring young people that it is not necessary to give up on God; in fact, He may empower them to think more clearly and rationally because of their faith.

But that doesn't mean it will always be smooth sailing. The great believer and thinker Joseph Smith said, "A fanciful and flowery and heated imagination beware of, because the things of God are of deep import, and time, and experience, and careful, and solemn, and ponderous thoughts can only find them out."[6]

The Difference between God and Santa Claus

As we talk to teenagers about God, we have to find a way of separating fact from fiction. Ironically, one of the best ways to do this is to have them read a lot of fiction. As children, we were probably told fairy tales and mythological stories. Such stories are an important part of every culture; these legends help children come to terms with all of the unseen dangers of existence. When we were little, we simply believed in Santa, the Tooth Fairy, and the boogeyman right along with Jesus Christ and the Holy Ghost. But at some point, we had to make a distinction between myth and faith. One of my students put the dilemma this way: "We have Greek myths, old legends, fictional stories, and the Bible with its Eden and ark and flood and plagues. What is the difference between the false stories and the true ones?"

The difference can be illustrated with God and Santa Claus. When we were children, we believed that Santa would bring us gifts if we are good. Unfortunately, many adults have not progressed beyond the childish view of God as a sort of Santa Claus, and they grow bitter and angry if God doesn't bring them the things on their list. (In fact, behind many of the cynical, sophisticated philosophies about life and its lack of meaning, we can feel the hurt and anger of the child who, though "worthy," didn't get what they expected out of life.) But, as Paul told us, there comes a time to stop thinking like a child and put away childish things.

God isn't Santa Claus, and the Book of Mormon makes that point in big, bold statements. God is a loving being, but He is great and powerful and far more complex than we can understand as children. Samuel told us that we are not going to "get away" with anything. Whatever we do, whether good or bad, we do to ourselves. "And now remember, remember, my brethren, that whosoever perisheth, perisheth unto himself; and whosoever doeth iniquity, doeth it unto himself; for behold, ye are free; ye are permitted to act for yourselves; for behold, God hath given unto you a knowledge and he hath made you free" (Helaman 14:30).

Behold, Is This Not Real?

So what's the difference between the Book of Mormon stories and fictional tales? The difference is in their power. Unlike the wishful thinking in myths and fairy tales, there is an actual moving power behind the events in the Book of Mormon. It's like the difference between a model of a car and one with a real engine. When you push on the gas pedal of a car, it lurches forward; it has power. It can take you somewhere—or it can even run over you, but it's real. Santa is a story; God is really there. When God acts, things happen, though we don't always understand them. This is why missionaries don't have to "sell" the gospel. They only have to hand over the key to the car by inviting people to get on their knees and pray about the scriptures. When they do so in faith, the car lurches forward and starts to move, and the awed investigator hangs on for the ride.

If you pray to Santa, you end up with a story. If you pray to God, a new power is unleashed into your life. As Alma said, "Is not this real?" (Alma 32:35). It is. When we open the Book of Mormon and read it together with our teenagers, we can help them unleash its power into their own lives, and thus give them the tools to live the righteous, joyful lives: "Therefore, blessed are they who will repent and hearken unto the voice of the Lord their God; for these are they that shall be saved" (Helaman 12:23).

The Big, Round Characters in the Book of Mormon

In writing, something often discussed is the difference between *round* characters and *flat* characters. In fiction, a flat character is basically a set of actions. Little is known about the character's inner, driving motivations, basically being all bad, all good, or all some other one thing. Escapist literature abounds in such characters; they serve to move the plot along and give us comfortable, "we know where this is going and we won't have to work hard to get there" feelings.

A round character, by contrast, feels fully human. Though we might easily identify him or her as the hero or the villain of a story, he or she will also surprise us somehow. Heroes might make errors in judgment or even terrible mistakes that make us question whether they can really be labeled heroes anymore. Villains might show unexpected compassion or feel terribly conflicted. We might be given insights into the backstories of the characters, making us feel more empathetic and less likely to use convenient labels. These confusing, complex, human characters are crucial components of great literature. Through them, we view ourselves in a new way.

The Book of Mormon introduces over a hundred characters; some appear in just a few verses and some spend a good deal of time with us. At least twenty of these are fully fleshed out, round characters who offer us an opportunity to view our life experiences through the eyes of another.

Notes

1. Joseph E Ucsinski and Joseph M. Parent, *American Conspiracy Theories* (New York: Oxford University Press, 2014), 3.

2. Seth Balfour, *Conspiracy Theories: The Controversial Stories, Deception and Beliefs of Our World's Most Mystifying Conspiracy Theories* (2015).

3. Gordon B. Hinckley, "The Times in Which We Live," *Ensign*, November 2001.

4. Gordon B. Hinckley, as quoted in Dallin H. Oaks, "Preparation for the Second Coming," *Ensign*, May 2004.

5. David Dobbs, "Beautiful Brains," *National Geographic* Magazine, October 2011.

6. Joseph Smith, *Teachings of the Prophet Joseph Smith* (Salt Lake City: Deseret Book, 1976), 137.

Your Stories and Thoughts

3 Nephi: Jesus Christ Changes Everything

In Our Midst: Finding Jesus in the Temple (3 Nephi 11)

Whenever a story takes place in or near the temple, it's interesting to see if there is something about it that directly relates to our own modern experiences in the temple. Jacob's discourse (given at the temple) contained many elements of our temple covenants, and King Benjamin's sermon echoed it almost exactly. In the marvelous climax of this nearly thousand-year history, Christ chose to meet His people at the temple. Many elements of our temple worship can be found in the record of His visit.

A few years before the birth of Christ, Samuel the Lamanite stood up on a city wall and preached about the signs of Jesus's coming. The signs of His birth did appear, but they were followed by thirty-three long years when nothing was known of the Savior. The Nephite society went through various upheavals, and then, when hope was nearly lost, the signs of Jesus's death and Resurrection occurred, including the destruction of many cities at the time of His Crucifixion. Finally, a still small voice was heard, proclaiming His coming, and Jesus Himself descended into the midst of the people, and they became acquainted with Him over the course of many days.

Jesus's visit to the Nephites was a part of His forty-day ministry, between His Resurrection and His final Ascension into heaven. LDS scholars agree that it was during this time that Jesus revealed the higher ordinances to His disciples. John Welch stated, "Jesus only had a short time to spend with these people at the temple at Bountiful. He didn't waste a word. What he says is of crucial importance. It's the kind of thing that you and I can look to as an anchor in our lives to put our bearings straight, . . . and to see what really matters most in our covenant relationship with our Father in Heaven."[1]

Jesus Meets His People at the Temple

The fact that Jesus meets His people at the temple is significant, for it is through the temple covenants that we step into a new relationship with Him. We wait until we're adults to go to the temple for a reason; this is a crucial time on life's path—the phase where many people give up on faith altogether. This loss of innocence is the stuff of literature, and it is also a theme in the temple. Adam and Eve had to decide whether to cling to innocence or choose experience. Their courageous choices show us, however, that the loss of innocence need not signal a descent into sin. We can move from innocence to experience, from childhood faith to spiritual maturity, by making and keeping covenants with Christ. Thus, the temple has been given to us, not as one more thing on our to-do list, but as a vehicle for spiritual rebirth. It is through covenants that our efforts to keep the commandments meet the grace of Christ.

As we go through the worship services at the temple, we experience many of the same things that the Nephites did. We are blessed and taught, and we experience sacred moments of prayer. The culmination recalls the beautiful moment when Jesus invited each person present to come and receive a personal witness of His redeeming grace:

> And it came to pass that the Lord spake unto them saying: Arise and come forth unto me, that ye may thrust your hands into my side, and also that ye may feel the prints of the nails in my hands and in my feet, that ye may know that I am the God of Israel, and the God of the whole earth, and have been slain for the sins of the world. And it came to pass that the multitude went forth, and thrust their hands into his side, and did feel the prints of the nails in his hands and in

his feet; and this they did do, going forth *one by one* until they had all gone forth, and did see with their eyes and did feel with their hands, and did know of a surety and did bear record, that it was he, of whom it was written by the prophets, that should come. (3 Nephi 11:13–15; emphasis added)

Jesus's appearance to the Nephites is replayed, symbolically, in every session of temple worship; the same joy the Nephites felt is available to all of us if we just do as they did—look up: "And it came to pass, as they understood they cast their eyes up again towards heaven; and behold, they saw a Man descending out of heaven; and he was clothed in a white robe; and he came down and stood in the midst of them" (3 Nephi 11:8).

Sometimes, in the press of the many responsibilities we have in life, it's easy to miss the joy that Jesus offers, the sense that He is actually here in the midst of us. The temple allows us a quiet place and time to concentrate on the relationship we are building with Him though our covenants. We can pray for angels to attend our loved ones and receive the power that is promised us as we are faithful. We can rehearse, in a small measure, what it will be like to meet Him again one day and hear Him whisper (in that still small voice), "Welcome home."

The Glorious Resurrection versus the Zombie Apocalypse (3 Nephi 12–16)

The book of 3 Nephi has been called the "fifth Gospel." One of the strongest features of this book is the testimony it offers of a literal, physical resurrection. The first thing the Savior did after He descended into the midst of the people was affirm the reality of His death and Resurrection. He wanted every person there to know that He was, in fact, the same person who died on Calvary's cross. It wasn't enough for just a few people to touch Him; He wanted every single person there to feel the sacred marks of His sacrifice.

> And it came to pass that the Lord spake unto them saying: Arise and come forth unto me, that ye may thrust your hands into my side, and also that ye may feel the prints of the nails in my hands and in my feet, that ye may know that I am the God of Israel, and the God of the whole earth, and have been slain for the sins of the world. And it came to pass that the multitude went forth, and thrust their hands into his side, and did feel the prints of the nails in his hands and in his feet; and this they did do, *going forth one by one until they had all gone forth*, and did see with their eyes and did feel with their hands, and did know of a surety and did bear record, that it was he, of whom it was written by the prophets, that should come. (3 Nephi 11:13–15; emphasis added)

From the Risen Christ to Vampires and Zombies

These days, the undead are all the rage. The incredible popularity of the Twilight series of vampire novels (and their movie versions) was just the beginning—zombies were next! One of the most watched shows on television is *The Walking Dead*, now in its sixth grim season. Its dark tone and graphic violence attract million of viewers per episode, who find it entertaining to watch corpse-like creatures feed on flesh.[2] What is it about vampires and zombies and such that's so appealing?

In his book *Monsters in America*, W. Scott Poole theorized, "The zombies of popular culture are situated in the trajectory of American history . . . [as] the zombie symbolizes for many Americans the current state of their own society or its eventual direction. The hopelessness of the genre, with its images of civilization's dissolution, and human beings cannibalizing one another . . . points to a profound unease about current American society and its place in global history." Poole described the zombie craze as a "subversive reimagining of Christian eschatology," taking one of the central symbols of Christianity, the resurrection of the dead, and turning it into a "symbol of sacrilege."[3]

Popular Christian commentator Eric Metaxas pointed to a comment made by one of the characters in the Walking Dead series, described as a "man of faith": "I can't profess to understand God's plan," this character said. "Christ promised the resurrection of the dead. I just thought he had something a little different in mind."[4]

Feeding on Hopelessness

Fans of the undead genre seem to see no harm in enjoying such horrific fictional journeys on a regular basis. It's useful to understand that this position is not new. Through his servants, the adversary has promoted horror and hopelessness as long as there have been people to deceive. Three of his greatest proponents appear in the Book of Mormon as the three anti-Christs: Sherem, Nehor, and Korihor. All three put forth arguments we hear today, but in particular Korihor sounds extra up-to-date, asserting that because we can't know anything for sure, it's silly to organize our lives around "pretended mysteries" that enslave the common people: "Yea, they durst not make use of that which is their own lest they should offend their priests, who do yoke them according to their desires, and have brought them to believe, by their traditions and their dreams and their whims and their visions and their pretended mysteries, that they should, if they did not do according to their words, offend some unknown being, who they say is God—a being who never has been seen or known, who never was nor ever will be" (Alma 30:28).

Humans deplore vacuums, so such are quickly filled with superstition. This can certainly be seen in the resurgence of interest in vampires, zombies, and other mythical creatures. In his seminal work *Religion and the Decline of Magic*, Keith Thomas defined magic as "the employment of ineffective techniques to allay anxiety when effective ones are not available."[5] In other words, when people have let go of the effective truths of the gospel, the ineffective ones of magic and superstition quickly take their place.

The Resurrection: A Shocking Event

Christ's Resurrection was surely the most surprising event ever to happen, and as soon as it happened, it became the center of debate. The different Gospel writers all chronicled the Resurrection somewhat differently, but one thing is certain—all agreed that it was not an imaginary event. Each of them emphasized the physical reality of Jesus's Resurrection. He shared meals, walked, talked, and held the disciples. And above all, He showed the marks of His Crucifixion to them so that they would know that He was the same person they had placed in the tomb. Today, however, many Christian scholars deny the physical Resurrection, claiming instead that the Resurrection was an oral tradition that grew to gain converts. Bart Ehrman represents this group when he said if you can't prove it, you can't believe in it.

> What about the resurrection of Jesus? I'm not saying it didn't happen; but if it did happen, it would be a miracle. The resurrection claims are claims that not only that Jesus's body came back alive; it came back alive never to die again. That's a violation of what naturally happens, every day, time after time, millions of times a year. What are the chances of that happening? Well, it'd be a miracle. In other words, it'd be so highly improbable that we can't account for it by natural means. . . . By the very nature of the canons of historical research, we can't claim historically that a miracle probably happened. By definition, it probably didn't.[6]

You Can Count on It

Jesus was resurrected, and it was a miracle. All of us will rise again someday and be reunited with our bodies. When we believe in the literal resurrection, all of life is filled with hope and joy that is otherwise lost to us. The "fifth Gospel," 3 Nephi, is a crowning testament of that reality and joins the other Gospels in proclaiming the good news.

But the Book of Mormon goes further than just recounting the visit of Christ to the Nephites. Every prophet, from Lehi to Moroni, testified of the literal Resurrection. Jacob said that the prophets of old knew of His coming as well, though their records had been diminished over time. "Behold, they believed in Christ and worshiped the Father in his name, and also we worship the Father in his name. . . . We are not witnesses alone in these things; for God also spake them unto prophets of old" (Jacob 4:5, 13).

Christ listed His Atonement, death, and Resurrection as the very definition of the gospel (see 3 Nephi 26:13). If we treat the Resurrection as simply a hopeful myth, its power is lost, and we are left with a superstitious fascination with everything that seems to conquer death but really only distracts us from the true source of life. As we embrace the reality of the Resurrection, its power reaches into our lives, filling us with a hope and an eternal optimism that infuses this life with joy.

The Sacrament and the Covenant Christian (3 Nephi 17–18)

What does it mean to be born again? The term *born again* is used to describe a conversion to Christ that brings a person into a state of grace, or of being "saved."[7] Latter-day Saints are sometimes uncomfortable with that definition because it seems to imply that a life of obedience to the commandments isn't required. There really isn't a satisfactory resolution to this debate, and getting involved in it can distract us from the real point, which is that each of us must personally decide what it means to be born again. The Book of Mormon offers some important insights about this.

A climactic moment in the Book of Mormon comes in 3 Nephi 17, as Jesus prepared to depart. The people, as one, were so filled with longing that He agreed to stay a little longer, blessing and ministering to them. Jesus blessed their children, healed their sick, and sent angels to minister to them. He prayed for them to His Father in such a powerful way that their hearts nearly burst for joy. This not only illustrates the intensely personal relationship that Christ offers us, but what comes next gives us an idea of how that relationship can grow.

Immediately following this incredible outpouring of the Spirit, Christ sent the disciples off to find wine and bread, had the multitude sit down, and instituted the ordinance of the sacrament. He did it twice, repeating it the next day when thousands more had gathered to see Him. In each case, a joyful, emotional connection with the Lord is made official with a covenant.

Becoming a Covenant Christian

Covenant-making as a sign of rebirth through the Spirit is a recurring theme in the Book of Mormon. King Benjamin's people experienced a great rebirth and immediately entered into a covenant, taking upon themselves the name of Christ. In another passage, Alma instructed his little flock about the baptismal covenant, and they joyfully accepted that commitment. Later, when Jesus Himself instituted the sacrament among the ancient American people, He explained that "it shall be a testimony unto the Father that ye do always remember me" (3 Nephi 18:7).

Jesus told the people that the sacrament is a central component in the Christian life, for "this doth witness unto the Father that ye are willing to do that which I have commanded you" (3 Nephi 18:10). The sacrament is the sign of our covenant with Christ, and when we partake of the sacrament, we are renewing our vow of love and obedience to Him.

Just as there is a great difference between a person who claims to be in love and a person who enters into the commitment of marriage, the covenant of baptism and its weekly repetition through the sacrament shows the difference between a person who simply believes and a person who is truly a Christian.

President Henry B. Eyring said, "The Latter-day Saints are a covenant people. From the day of baptism through the spiritual milestones of our lives, we make promises with God and He makes promises with us. He *always* keeps His promises offered through His authorized servants, but it is the crucial test of our lives to see if *we* will make and keep our covenants with Him."[8]

Covenants are the key to bringing consistency to our Christianity; they transform a loving impulse into a long-term relationship with the Savior. Our covenants anchor us to Him and offer a center for our spiritual lives. When Alma asks us, "Have ye spiritually been born of God?" (Alma 5:14), we can confidently answer "Yes, and not only have I been born of God, I am also in a covenant relationship with Him that will last until He welcomes me safely home." That is the security Christ offers us—the knowledge that He never fails to honor His promises and will always be there as we enter into covenants with Him.

This Is the Gospel: Why Everybody Needs a Savior (3 Nephi 26–27)

While studying Japanese at the Language Training Mission in Hawaii, I attended a stake conference that I have never forgotten. A beautiful teenage girl was giving a talk on the gospel of Jesus Christ. Suddenly, she turned to a visiting General Authority and invited him to join her at the podium and asked him to define the gospel in one sentence.

He smiled and gave a nice summation, including perfecting the Saints, redeeming the dead, and proclaiming the gospel to the world. She smiled back and gently told him, "No, that is not what Jesus says." Then she opened to the book of 3 Nephi and read,

> Behold I have given unto you my gospel, and *this is the gospel* which I have given unto you—that I came into the world to do the will of my Father, because my Father sent me. And my Father sent me that I might be lifted up upon the cross; and after that I had been lifted up upon the cross, that I might draw all men unto me, that as I have been lifted up by men even so should men be lifted up by the Father, to stand before me, to be judged of their works, whether they be good or whether they be evil—and for this cause have I been lifted up; therefore, according to the power of the Father I will draw all men unto me, that they may be judged according to their works. (3 Nephi 26:13–15; emphasis added)

We were all humbled by this sweet young woman and her simple definition of the gospel, taken right from the Savior Himself. I had occasion to remember that experience just six months later when I received my first assignment as a senior companion and was sent by my mission president to the beautiful city of Fukushima, Japan (tragically, the site of the 2011 nuclear disaster). President Teruya explained to me in his optimistic way that, though sisters had never served in Fukushima, he was sending us there specifically to convert one person. "Her name is Sister Hayakawa," he said. "Her husband is the elder's quorum president, and I want to call him to be the branch president, but she is not a member. She's been through several sets of missionaries and now she won't even let the elders in the door. So you girls go down there and bring her into the Church, okay?"

Oh, President Teruya had such a way of making things sound simple! My new companion, Sister Hamasaki, and I went down to Fukushima, set up housekeeping, and (when we couldn't put it off any longer) finally went trembling to the door of the Hayakawa home. Sister Hayakawa was so surprised to meet female missionaries that she let us in. My companion and I had been praying about what to teach her, because we knew we probably only had one shot, and we both felt impressed that we should go right to the heart of the gospel and teach about the Savior. I used the theme from that stake conference I attended in Hawaii—that the Atonement of Jesus Christ *is* the gospel.

Why Do I Need a Savior?

Sister Hayakawa listened politely as we explained the laws of justice and mercy and how the Atonement paid for our sins. Then she smiled and said, "Yes, I find your Western concept of sin interesting. But I am Japanese, not Western. We do not believe in sin the way you do, so I don't need a Savior. I am kind to others and do not knowingly hurt people. I am a good wife and mother. I understand why people who make serious mistakes need a Savior, but I don't. If I don't believe in sin, why do I need a Savior?"

I've never been asked a more challenging question in my life. Sister Hayakawa's question has relevance to us all, for though Latter-day Saints recognize the Savior as the Son of God, we may not feel that His redeeming power reaches us on a daily basis. So why do we need a Savior every day?

There are a few moments in the Book of Mormon where people really get it, and it usually involves opening their eyes. The people of King Benjamin, under the influence of the Spirit, "viewed themselves in their own carnal state, even less than the dust of the earth" (Mosiah 4:2). Alma the Younger "saw that I had rebelled against my God" (Alma 36:13). And, as the Savior descended into their midst, "the eyes of the whole multitude were turned upon him" (3 Nephi 11:8).

How could I help Sister Hayakawa see the need for a Savior? How do we help our children, or those we are trying to teach, feel the need for the Savior's redeeming grace?

The Answer Is in Our Own Hearts

I learned that day that we don't need scholarship or great presentation skills to convey the truth to others. We just need the Savior to open our eyes. It came into my mind to ask Sister Hayakawa, "Have you ever done anything of which you are ashamed, that you wish would just go away? Have you ever done damage to or hurt another person in a way you wish you could undo? If you knew that feeling of shame and regret could be erased forever, would you welcome that?" I could see that this question hit the mark and her heart was touched. Of course she needed a Savior. Everyone needs Him, whether they know about Him or not. Once her eyes were opened to her need for a Savior, Sister Hayakawa was ready to hear the gospel message.

Every step we take through life, our progression is made possible by the Atonement of Christ. When Jesus said, "I will draw all men unto me" (3 Nephi 27:15), He is talking about a real, compelling power that pulls us toward Him. And it always involves seeing things more clearly than we did before. C. S. Lewis said, "The beauty of the Atonement is like the beauty of the sunrise, in that we not only enjoy it for itself, but by the light of it we see the beauty of everything else."⁹

A few years ago, I went back to Japan after an absence of almost four decades. Craig and I spent the night with the Hayakawas, who have been pillars in the Church there for thirty-five years. The little boy who played on the floor while we taught the discussions came to dinner with his wife and three children; he is the bishop of the ward. The light that lit up Sister Hayakawa's face the day we talked about the Savior hasn't dimmed, and the peace that she shares with her husband and family is the hope in Christ that gives life to the soul. This is the gospel—that He came to draw us all to Him through His redeeming love.

Notes

1. John Welch, as quoted in Hugh W. Nibley, *Nibley's Commentary on the Book of Mormon* (Provo, Utah: Foundation for Ancient Research and Mormon Studies, 2004), 128.

2. See https://en.wikipedia.org/wiki/Template:The_Walking_Dead_ratings.

3. W. Scott Poole, *Monsters in America* (Waco, Texas: Baylor University Press, 2011), 217.

4. See Eric Metaxas, *Breakpoint*, http://www.breakpoint.org/bpcommentaries/entry/13/23793.

5. Keith Thomas, *Religion and the Decline of Magic* (London: Penguin Books, 1971), 800.

6. William Lane Craig and Bart D. Ehrman, "Is There Historical Evidence for the Resurrection of Jesus?" College of the Holy Cross, March 2006, http://www.philvaz.com/apologetics/p96.htm.

7. "In some Christian movements (especially Fundamentalism and Evangelicalism), to be *born again* is to undergo a 'spiritual rebirth,' or a regeneration of the human spirit from the Holy Spirit." See "Born again (Christianity)," *Wikipedia*, https://en.wikipedia.org/wiki/Born_again_%28Christianity%29.

8. Henry B. Eyring, "Witnesses for God," *Ensign*, November 1996, 30.

9. C. S. Lewis, *The Complete C. S. Lewis Signature Classics* (New York: HarperCollins Publishers, 2002).

Your Stories and Thoughts

4 Nephi: Living after the Manner of Happiness

Where Is the Happiest Place on Earth? (4 Nephi 1)

The high point in the Book of Mormon occurs in the century that follows Christ's visit to the Nephites. After all of the tumult surrounding His Crucifixion, the Lord Himself came and spent an extended amount of time with this remnant of the Israelites. After His Ascension into heaven, a time of peace and prosperity ensued that last for nearly two hundred years. Here's how Mormon described it: "And it came to pass that there was no contention in the land, because of the love of God which did dwell in the hearts of the people. And there were no envyings, nor strifes, nor tumults, nor whoredoms, nor lyings, nor murders, nor any manner of lasciviousness; and surely there could not be a happier people among all the people who had been created by the hand of God" (4 Nephi 1:15–16).

Inevitably, cracks and fissures began to appear in the solid, happy foundation that had been established by the Savior. Those cracks were first manifest in the separation of people into classes based on their affluence. Mormon wrote that in the beginning, they had all things in common and finally gave up the tribal distinctions of Nephites, Lamanites, and so on. In one of my favorite passages in the book, he said that there "were no robbers, nor murderers, neither were there Lamanites, nor any manner of -ites; but they were in one, the children of Christ, and heirs to the kingdom of God" (4 Nephi 1:17).

Again, he repeated how blessed and happy the people were, and how this condition lasted until almost two hundred years had passed. And then money crept into the picture. As some became more affluent, they no longer wanted to have all things in common. "And they began to be divided into classes" (4 Nephi 1:26).

Why Can't We Be Satisfied with Happiness?

As Mormon describes the wonderful state of the Nephite society, I can't help but wonder: Why couldn't they have just been happy being happy? Why do people undermine their own well-being? If human beings are meant to be happy, why don't they recognize it when it happens and just enjoy it? In his book *Happiness Is a Serious Problem*, Dennis Prager asserted that "human beings are insatiable." In other words, no matter how much we have, something inside of us quickly becomes dissatisfied with that and establishes a new benchmark by which to measure happiness. Once we recognize that about ourselves, we can take steps to control the beast of insatiability. "Because human nature is insatiable our brain, with its rational and philosophical abilities, not our nature, must be the arbiter of whether we are happy. We must be able, in effect, to tell our nature that although we hear it and respect it, our mind, not our nature, will determine whether we are satisfied."[1]

Easier said than done, isn't it? The vague feeling of "unhappiness" has led to more sorrow and sin than can be measured. Marriages end, children rebel, and addictions begin with that insatiable desire for something more that seems to be lacking in life. The book of 4 Nephi is a great reminder to all that, even if you had everything you ever dreamed of, there would be something inside of you wanting more.

But we can be happy right now in whatever circumstance we may find ourselves by enlisting the help of the Lord. We can learn to see and appreciate what is right around us and avoid the deception that we need more to be happy. Victor Frankl, who survived the horrors of the concentration camps and went on to inspire millions, reminded us that "happiness cannot be pursued; it must ensue." Happiness is a byproduct of living a life that has meaning and purpose. He further advised,

> Don't aim at success. The more you aim at it and make it a target, the more you are going to miss it. For success, like happiness, cannot be pursued; it must ensue, and it only does so as the unintended side effect of one's personal dedication to a cause greater than oneself or as the by-product of one's surrender to a person other than oneself. Happiness must happen, and the same holds for success: you have to let it happen by not caring about it. I want you to listen to what your conscience commands you to do and go on to carry it out to the best of your knowledge. Then you will live to see that in the long-run—in the long-run, I say!—success will follow you precisely because you had forgotten to think about it. . . . Once an individual's search for a meaning is successful, it not only renders him happy but also gives him the capability to cope with suffering.[2]

We're meant to be happy, but happiness comes from meaning and purpose. When the byproduct became the object, the people lost it, and the Nephite society began its final, tragic decline. What a lesson for each of us. Are we seeking "happiness" or a life of meaning and purpose?

The Parable of the Perfect Circle (4 Nephi)

Once there was group of people who experienced one magnificent event together—a lengthy visit from the Savior Himself. Over the course of several days, Christ taught them the gospel, prayed with them, healed them, and invited them to touch the tokens of His sacrifice in His hands and feet. Their children were encircled about by holy fire, and angels ministered to them; they experienced a little of heaven on earth. It was a perfect circle of love.

Because of these experiences, the people were united and righteous for two hundred years. Again, the scriptures state, "And it came to pass that there was no contention in the land, because of the love of God which did dwell in the hearts of the people. And there were no envyings, nor strifes, nor tumults, nor whoredoms, nor lyings, nor murders, nor any manner of lasciviousness; and surely there could not be a happier people among all the people who had been created by the hand of God" (4 Nephi 1:15–16).

Encircled in the Arms of His Love

When the pioneers were crossing the plains, at night they pulled the wagons into a circle as a protection against enemies. In the same way, animals form a circle around one that is ailed or injured. A circle is a position of strength—it allows each member to be supported on each side, and no one is left vulnerable to attack. It isn't surprising that a circle is the ideal configuration for prayer.

When the San Diego California Temple was completed in 1993, four of our five children were old enough to attend the dedicatory service. We were lucky enough to sit in the celestial room for the service. When it was over, we gathered them into a circle and, with our arms around each other, we promised that we would all meet back in that room someday for their weddings. The feeling we had that day was, I think, something close to what the Nephites experienced. It was an almost perfect joy.

Sadly, sometimes life gets in the way of that peace, and the circle can be broken. That is when we need to reexamine our lives and see where the cracks are forming.

Our family circles begin to crack when fighting, contention, pride, and prejudice creep into our lives. Any time we throw out insults, blame, or criticism at a family member, we cause a little crack in our perfect circle. On the other hand, every time we say kind and loving words, show support for each other, or express love in any way, we wrap a golden flaxen cord around the circle and strengthen it.

If we imitate the things that Jesus did with the Nephites—prayer, blessings, teaching, and loving time together—we can build the family circle. Remember, whatever you do or say either strengthens or weakens it. Keep the circle strong enough to gather everyone safely inside it again in the Lord's good time.

Notes

1. Dennis Prager, *Happiness Is a Serious Problem: A Human Nature Repair Manual* (New York: Regan Books, 1998).

2. Viktor E. Frankl, *Goodreads*, http://www.goodreads.com/quotes/34673-don-t-aim-at-success-the-more-you-aim-at-it.

Your Stories and Thoughts

Mormon: The Keeper of the Record

Mormon's Lament: Why Is Life So Hard? (Mormon 6)

The Book of Mormon is a tragic narrative; the people who started so optimistically in the New World are, in the end, defeated by the divisions that sprang up in the first weeks of their exodus. Yet it is also a triumphant story because, along the way, many of God's children had the opportunity to know and live the gospel and enjoy a hope in Christ. The overarching narrative of the book is mirrored in the life of Mormon.

Mormon first received his calling as the record keeper at the age of ten, when he was commanded to wait until he turned twenty-four, and then recover the buried records and complete the plates of Nephi. At fifteen, he became a military leader and, with all of the social upheavals, he was thirty-five before he was finally able to return to the hiding place of the records and create his abridgement of them.

His task was a big one—after transcribing Nephi's record, Mormon narrated the history of the Nephites, starting two hundred years before Christ's birth and going right up until his own day four hundred years after Christ's coming. Mormon was seventy-four when he finally completed his project and passed it to his son Moroni. So we can see that Mormon's life, like Nephi's, was bookended by his responsibility to the sacred record. This would've been hard to foresee when he first received his charge as a young boy.

Why Is Life So Hard?

Mormon's life was full of service and accomplishments, but his was also a really sad and difficult existence. He was forced to witness such depravity among his own people that he didn't want to record it. "And now behold, I, Mormon, do not desire to harrow up the souls of men in casting before them such an awful scene of blood and carnage as was laid before mine eyes" (Mormon 5:8). He described himself as being "without hope" that things could get better. He spent his last days mourning the decline of his people: "O ye fair sons and daughters, ye fathers and mothers, ye husbands and wives, ye fair ones, how is it that ye could have fallen! But behold, ye are gone, and my sorrows cannot bring your return" (Mormon 6:19–20).

Mormon's life teaches us something about our own; namely, we can't always be happy. Though we may make right decisions, we will endure many tragic events through no fault of our own. For everyone, even the most fortunate, joy and sadness will inevitably be bound up together. As William Blake wrote,

> Joy and woe are woven fine,
> A clothing for the soul divine.
> Under every grief and pine
> Runs a joy with silken twine. . . .
> It is right it should be so;
> Man was made for joy and woe;
> And when this we rightly know,
> Thro' the world we safely go.[1]

Well, why does life have to be so hard? In his bestselling book *The Road Less Traveled*, M. Scott Peck began with a devastatingly simple sentence: "Life is difficult."[2] This seems like an obvious truth, but we tend to react with surprise and disappointment when challenges and obstacles spring up in our paths. Peck continued, "Most do not fully see this truth that life is difficult. Instead they moan more or less incessantly, noisily or subtly, about the enormity of their problems, their burdens, and their difficulties, as if life were generally easy, as if life *should* be easy. . . . I know about this . . . because I have done my share."[3]

Is Your Story Tragic or Triumphant?

What are our lives really about? Sometimes it's hard to say. In his novel about the Old Testament prophet Joseph, Thomas Mann had Joseph say to his brothers at their tearful reunion, "In asking for my forgiveness, you have not, it appears, really understood the whole story we are in. I do not scold you for that. One can very easily be in a story without understanding it. Perhaps it was meant to be that way."[4]

Our preconceived notions about what our lives ought to be like can keep us from understanding what we have actually been given. We each have a life story that includes certain responsibilities, specific duties, and spiritual stewardships. We can get so caught up in asking why things aren't working out as we expected that we rationalize taking easier roads rather than giving our full effort to our appointed tasks.

Mormon may not have fully understand the story he was in, but he had perfect faith in its Author—he understood his duty. His single-hearted commitment to follow, step by step, the guidance of the Spirit can be seen by how carefully he inquired of the Lord about what to record and what to omit and by his many side notes to us, his unseen audience. His was a great example of a soul whose life was not happy or easy, but whose mission was successful. His lament over his people tears at the heart: "And my soul was rent with anguish, because of the slain of my people, and I cried: O ye fair ones, how could ye have departed from the ways of the Lord! O ye fair ones, how could ye have rejected that Jesus, who stood with open arms to receive you!" (Mormon 6:16–17).

Yet at the end of his life, as he passed the record to his son, Mormon had perfect peace about the part he had been asked to play. This is his poignant summation of his life, one we might hope to emulate, no matter what life throws our way: "Behold, a continual scene of wickedness and abominations has been before mine eyes ever since I have been sufficient to behold the ways of man. And wo is me because of their wickedness; for my heart has been filled with sorrow because of their wickedness, all my days; nevertheless, I know that I shall be lifted up at the last day" (Mormon 2:18–19).

Mormon's Unique Voice

Nephi and Mormon are the two major narrators of the Book of Mormon, and each has a unique voice. Mormon was largely a historian at heart; he included specific dates wherever he could. Like Matthew in the Gospels, he framed his narrative as a fulfillment of ancient prophecies.

In the course of the Book of Mormon, he interrupted the narrative over a hundred times to point our attention to certain things that he wanted us to notice, whether it was the hand of God in certain events or his own choices as narrator and redactor. Mormon often let us know that there is much more material that he wished he could've shared but was not able to, either for lack of space or (in the case of Jesus's third sermon to the Nephites) because he was forbidden by the Lord to record it.

Armies of Angels: Why It Makes Sense to Believe in Miracles (Mormon 9)

In fiction, we expect miraculous things to happen. Jane Eyre hears her soul mate's voice at the moment she is about to commit herself to another man. Oliver Twist is caught "stealing" from his own lost grandfather, and it leads to his physical, spiritual, and physical redemption. All of those characters in Shakespeare's comedies (I can't keep them straight) stumble over each other in the dark forest or in far-distant cities and get happily reunited. The coincidence, the *deus ex machina*, the sudden joyous turn (as Tolkein described it) is at the heart of fiction. Just when there's no hope, something amazing happens, and everyone lives happily ever after.

I contend that we love this quality in fiction because, in our hearts, we believe in real miracles. And, according to the Book of Mormon, belief is the magic ingredient that actually makes miracles happen. On this subject, Mormon quoted Moroni and Moroni quoted Mormon:

> I will show unto you a God of miracles . . . and the reason why he ceaseth to do miracles among the children of men is because that they dwindle in unbelief, and depart from the right way, and know not the God in whom they should trust. (Mormon 9:11, 20)

> Has the day of miracles ceased? Or have angels ceased to appear unto the children of men? . . . I say unto you, Nay; for it is by faith that miracles are wrought; . . . wherefore, if these things have ceased wo be unto the children of men, for it is because of unbelief, and all is vain. (Moroni 7:35–37)

In my experience, most people believe in miracles, though they may not be religious. Stop any person on the street and ask if anything miraculous has ever happened to them, and you'll hear a story. There is hardly a person who hasn't had something "stranger than fiction" happen in their "real" lives. Here are two miracles from my own experiences, one large and one small.

Big Miracle

Thirty-five years ago, I was studying Japanese in the Language Training Mission in Hawaii, and President Spencer W. Kimball gave a talk and called for more missionaries—thousands more, from all the countries of the world. He admitted that this would take a miracle, and then held up a picture of Sarah, laughing as she heard the holy men tell Abraham she would bear a son. In his gravelly voice, President Kimball said, "Is anything too hard for the Lord?" He called for missionaries to come out of every nation, to teach their own people.

To me, that seemed impossible at the time. When I arrived in the Sendai mission, I was assigned to the only Japanese sister. (There was a small handful of Japanese elders.) A month later, President Kimball came to Japan, and the Japanese missionaries went to hear him give this same talk in a stadium in Tokyo. All of my future Japanese companions heard him speak, and miracles happened in each of their lives that caused them to literally drop what they were doing and go on missions. For example, my next companion had attended that conference with her fiancé, and after the meeting they decided to take the money they had saved for their wedding and serve missions. At the end of my mission, there were twenty-eight Japanese sisters and around forty Japanese elders in our mission alone, one of six missions in Japan that all received that kind of influx. It was a miracle.

Small Miracle

Recently, I awoke early in the morning, unable to sleep. The app on my phone that lets me listen to the scriptures wasn't working, so in desperation I turned to the Mormon radio channel. There was a show on called *Why I Believe*, and a woman was telling the story of her conversion in Arkansas in 1972. I listened drowsily, and then suddenly my eyes snapped open as she repeated what her missionary, Elder Green, had said to her the first day she came to church and how she knew he spoke with God's inspiration, telling her something he couldn't himself have known.

I realized that she was talking about my brother, Alan. I was able to call him later and let him know that forty years after the event, his efforts in the mission field continued to bear fruit. What were the odds that I would awake in the night and tune into a station I never listen to, just in time to hear my brother mentioned so I could let him know that he was appreciated and loved for his service? It was small, but it was definitely a miracle.

When we talk about miracles, even small ones, we should mentally remove our shoes; we are on sacred ground. Unfortunately, many miracles go unnoticed or unacknowledged, and this is a shame because they're meant to be sudden sources of joy in a dark world. As we read stories that feature the unexpected but joyous turns of narrative that bring resolution to fictional characters, we are better prepared to appreciate the real miracles that happen in our own life narratives. As we recognize them, express gratitude for them, write them down, and share them with our children, miracles will increase in our lives—and so will our faith.

In the midst of the plagues of Egypt, there fell three days of darkness. Egyptians couldn't see a thing, and people were falling all over each other. But the scripture read, "All the children of Israel had light in their dwellings" (Exodus 10:23). One of the functions of great literature and the scriptures is to shed light in our dwellings in the midst of a dark world. Great fiction can lead us in the mental and spiritual exercise of opening what Charles Dickens called "our shut-up hearts"[5] and making room for the miraculous. With that as a starting point, a thoughtful faith can grow toward a perfect brightness, and when real miracles occur, we can recognize them for what they are: small beacons to light us on our journeys through a dark world until we arrive safely home.

Notes

1. William Blake, "Auguries of Innocence," *Bartleby*, http://www.bartleby.com/41/356.html.

2. M. Scott Peck, *The Road Less Traveled* (New York: Touchstone Books, 1978), 1.

3. Ibid.

4. Thomas Mann, *Joseph and His Brothers* (London: Everyman Library, 2005), 1491.

5. Charles Dickens, *A Christmas Carol* (London: Chapman & Hall, 1843).

Your Stories and Thoughts

Ether: The Power of One

Sixteen Stones: The Brother of Jared's Guide to Dating (Ether 2–3)

Everybody wants someone to love, and yet, as William Shakespeare observed, "The course of true love never did run smooth."[1] Of the prayers that ascend up nightly to heaven, I'd imagine that a significant percentage involve the search for or concerns about that one special person with whom one hopes to spend his or her life. Are you praying to find Mister or Miss Right? That's a pretty big request, but the brother of Jared actually has something to teach us about how to go about it.

A Man with No Name

The brother of Jared is a curious character in the Book of Mormon. His story is part of the record of the Jaredites, a group that came out of confusion surrounding the Tower of Babel. Jared's brother was clearly the spiritual giant of the group and went to the Lord on behalf of the people at Jared's behest. As a result, they were able to keep a common language amid the confusion and wandered as a group for about four years until God commanded them to make eight curious barges, in which they would cross the ocean.

The barges built, the brother of Jared asked the Lord about light, steering, and ventilation. The Lord explained how to provide ventilation and assured him that He would take care of the steering. But then the narrative takes an interesting turn. When the brother of Jared complained, "There is no light in them . . . wilt thou suffer that we shall cross this great water in darkness?" (Ether 2:22), the Lord handed the problem right back to him: "And the Lord said unto the brother of Jared: What will ye that I should do that ye may have light in your vessels?" The Lord went on to explain how the barges were designed to function like "a whale in the midst of the sea," alternately floating and submerged in the rolling waves, so any type of windows would be "dashed in pieces." "Therefore," the Lord repeated, "what will ye that I should prepare for you that ye may have light when ye are swallowed up in the depths of the sea?" (Ether 2:23–25).

The Ball's in Your Court

This fascinating story has much to teach about how prayer works. Sometimes, we think that if we just pray long and hard enough, God will give us what we ask, when, in reality, He may expect us to get creative and get to work. The brother of Jared gave the matter some thought, and then he took the initiative. "[He] did molten out of a rock sixteen small stones; and they were white and clear, even as transparent glass; and he did carry them in his hands upon the top of the mount, and cried again unto the Lord, saying . . . Touch these stones, O Lord, with thy finger, and prepare them that they may shine forth in darkness" (Ether 3:1, 4).

What do you want from the Lord? A sweetheart, a new job, or a better life for your family? Whatever you're praying for, can you count sixteen things that you have done to have that prayer come to pass? Let's think of sixteen things that a person could do to be more marriageable and divide them into four categories: spiritual, temporal, physical, and emotional. These sixteen stones are the same for men and women.

Sixteen Smooth Stones

Spiritual

1. Serve faithfully in a calling and attend church

2. Read your scriptures, pray, and attend the temple

3. Get rid of those secret sins you're hiding

4. Be more careful about what you take in via the media

Temporal

5. Get a career path, not just a job

6. Take care of your car and your living space

7. Spend at least a little money on dates—make things nice

8. Pay your tithing and be generous with others

Physical

9. Lose weight, tone up, and look your physical best

10. Get good advice about your hair and clothes and follow it

11. Be clean, wash your hair, and brush your tongue!

12. Brush up on your etiquette and show good manners

Emotional

13. Listen, show interest in others, and stop bragging

14. Surround yourself with positive people and be a positive person

15. Smile more and get offended less—lighten up!

16. Serve others, even when it doesn't benefit you

Now, these may not be your sixteen stones. You may have a different set, but you get the idea. We could just as easily make sixteen stones for getting a job or bettering our lifestyles. It's rare that we are proactively doing all that we need to do for the Lord to bless us with our desires. We might imagine that we hear the Lord saying to us, "What will ye that I should do?" (Ether 2:23). The secret to success for the brother of Jared was that he did sixteen things and asked the Lord for just one thing: to touch the stones with His finger. Imagine the increase in our faith if we could go to the Lord and say, "Look, I've done these sixteen things and prepared myself in every way I could think of to be the person I should be. Will you just touch me with your finger, so that I will 'shine forth in darkness' and my other half can find me?"

The brother of Jared combined two great qualities: creativity and pragmatism. He made it as easy as possible for the Lord to answer his prayer, and as a result his people crossed the waters with light in their vessels. Before we give up on the Lord and complain that our prayers aren't being answered, perhaps it might be worthwhile to make a list of sixteen things that we can do to help bring His blessings down on us.

This was only the beginning of the marvelous interactions between the Lord and the brother of Jared. "And they were taught to walk humbly before the Lord; and they were also taught from on high" (Ether 6:17). How much effort, time, and creativity are we willing to expend to receive His blessings? It takes quite a lot of effort to make molten glass out of stone sixteen times. But it was worth it to be touched with the light of Christ.

Study It Out in Your Mind

Joseph Smith worked with several scribes as he translated. First was Emma, his wife; Martin Harris and Oliver Cowdery followed her. It must have been quite an experience to act as the scribe and be the first to hear the words of the Book of Mormon. Oliver described it, "These were days never to be forgotten—to sit under the sound of a voice dictated by the inspiration of heaven, awakened the utmost gratitude of this bosom! Day after day I continued, uninterrupted, to write from his mouth, as he translated with the Urim and Thummim, or, as the Nephites would have said, 'Interpreters,' the history or record called 'The Book of Mormon.'"[2]

It would've been natural—especially for a bright, literate man like Oliver Cowdery—to begin to wonder if he, rather than Joseph Smith, might do a better job at translating. Oliver's desire to translate was granted, and then when he was unsuccessful, it was taken away. The Lord's counsel to him through Joseph Smith is relevant to the discussion about the brother of Jared and may give us some insight into the translation process used by Joseph Smith: "Behold, you have not understood; you have supposed that I would give it unto you, when you took no thought save it was to ask me. But, behold, I say unto you, that you must study it out in your mind; then you must ask me if it be right, and if it is right I will cause that your bosom shall burn within you; therefore, you shall feel that it is right" (D&C 9:7–8).

Confessions of a Wimp: A Discussion of Weakness (Ether 12)

"And if men come unto me I will show unto them their weakness. I give unto men weakness that they may be humble; and my grace is sufficient for all men that humble themselves before me; for if they humble themselves before me, and have faith in me, then will I make weak things become strong unto them" (Ether 12:27).

Alma introduced the word *infirmity* to us in relation to Christ's Atonement. Now in Ether, Mormon added depth to the dimensions of the Atonement in this discussion about weakness. You may find that, in your life (as in my life), weaknesses cause more pain to yourself and others than sins. Why are weaknesses so hard to overcome?

In her excellent book *Weakness Is Not a Sin*, Wendy Ulrich presented two simple yet intriguing ideas: Weakness and sin are very different and weakness and strength are not. Ulrich went on to explain that we often lump sin and weakness together, as if the first were just the natural extension of the second. Yet in reality, weakness is often the beginning of strength, as it stated in the above verse.[3] There is a consistent pattern in the scriptures—God using the weak to fulfill His purposes. Why?

How Do Weak Things Become Strong?

David and Goliath is the archetypal story of the triumph of the small and weak over the big and strong. In his book of the same name, Malcolm Gladwell pointed out that David's victory was due to the fact that he used his "weakness" rather than trying to imitate the strong man. When Saul tried to dress David in armor and hand him a sword, David instinctively knew what a mistake that would be. His weakness—the fact that he was young and small and had just a sling with stones—was also his strength. He was quick and agile and, in reality, quite deadly; a stone hurled from a sling by a skilled marksman has roughly the same impact as a bullet from a small handgun.[4]

Gladwell gave many examples of ways in which people have actually used what others would consider weakness to gain the advantage and succeed. This idea—that our weaknesses are not just impediments to be overcome but actually may be the keys to our greatest successes—can revolutionize our views of our life situations. For example, Gladwell cited a statistic that a disproportionate number of CEOs (as many as one in four) suffer from dyslexia. This indicates that there is something about dyslexia (a weakness) that can actually stimulate the qualities of a good CEO. He wrote, "Dyslexics are outsiders. . . . They are forced to stand apart from everyone else at school because they can't do the thing that school requires them to do. Is it possible for that 'outsiderness' to give them some kind of advantage down the line?"[5]

Compensation Learning versus Capitalization Learning

Gladwell used the terms *compensation* and *capitalization* to explain how most of us learn. We naturally gravitate toward the things we do well: natural singers take voice lessons and coordinated, husky boys play football. This is capitalization learning; we pursue areas in which we naturally excel. Compensation learning occurs when someone has a weakness (such as reading) and develops a new range of skills to compensate for that weakness. This often results in exceptionally strong people. Like resistance in weight training, the weakness actually enhances the overall strength.

How does this translate to our spiritual lives? Well, perhaps rather than continually berating ourselves for weaknesses, we might take a fresh look at them and see how, with God's help, they might be turned into strengths. Are you shy? Perhaps God can use that to help you be the best listener in your family. Are you prone to headaches or illness? Perhaps God can use that to help you be accessible and compassionate. In his beautiful autobiography *Flying without Wings*, psychiatrist Arnold Besser wrote of how tragedy transformed his life. He was the national amateur tennis champion completing his training as a surgeon when he was struck by polio—just months before the vaccine became available. He found himself in an iron lung, unable to move. His career derailed, his life was in danger, and he spent day after day simply looking at the ceiling, at the mercy of caregivers.

From this incredibly low point, Besser found a way to make his weakness his strength. Changing his specialty to psychiatry, Besser found that his disability made him uniquely accessible to people who were suffering. Rather than sitting and taking notes while people lay on his psychiatrist's couch, his respiratory problems forced him to lie down next to them. He sometimes even needed their help with his breathing apparatus. He found that people opened up to him in a way they wouldn't have otherwise done. His disability caused him to be filled with compassion and empathy for anyone paralyzed by any type of infirmity. His life has been an inspiration to thousands.[6]

Besser's willingness to share his weakness with others endears him to us. Though it's hard to share weaknesses with others, it can be the means to lifting their spirits. Philosopher Criss Jami said, "To share your weakness is to make yourself vulnerable; to make yourself vulnerable is to show your strength."[7]

What Is Your Hidden Strength?

My experience in life has been one more of weakness than strength. I seem to be continually tripping over my own weaknesses, especially when I have something important to do. When I hear people talk about the terrible trials they've faced, I'm reminded that the worst problems I have faced have been of my own making! Sometimes this has really gotten me down, but this section of scripture buoys me up. It reminds me that I can take a weakness (for example, I don't know when to shut up) and turn it into a strength (I'm a pretty good teacher). Rather than berate myself for the things that are wrong with me, I can try to exercise some *compensation* learning and make a silk purse out of that spiritual sow's ear.

So when we wonder why everything seems to go wrong when we're trying to do what's right, it may be worthwhile to remind ourselves that in God's logic, it makes heavenly sense to throw obstacles in our path when we're trying to do His work. Madeline L'Engle explained that those weaknesses can help us remember to lean on Him: "In a very real sense not one of us is qualified, but it seems that God continually chooses the most unqualified to do his work, to bear his glory. If we are qualified, we tend to think that we have done the job ourselves. If we are forced to accept our evident lack of qualification, then there's no danger that we will confuse God's work with our own, or God's glory with our own."[8]

Notes

1. William Shakespeare, *A Midsummer Night's Dream*, act one, scene one.

2. Oliver Cowdrey, published in Latter-day Saints' *Messenger and Advocate*, Vol. 1, No. 1, Kirtland, Ohio, October 1834.

3. Wendy Ulrich, *Weakness Is Not a Sin* (Salt Lake City: Deseret Book, 2009), 1.

4. Malcolm Gladwell, *David and Goliath: Underdogs, Misfits, and the Art of Battling Giants* (New York: Little, Brown and Company, 2013), 11.

5. Ibid., 115.

6. Arnold Besser, *Flying without Wings* (New York: Doubleday Books, 1988).

7. Criss Jami, *Goodreads*, http://www.goodreads.com/quotes/512034 -to-share-your-weakness-is-to-make-yourself-vulnerable-to.

8. Madeleine L'Engle, *Walking on Water: Reflections on Faith and Art* (New York: North Point Press, 1980), 62.

Your Stories and Thoughts

Moroni: Last Words from the Last Man Standing

Mormon's Four-Step Guide to Perfect Parenting (Moroni 7)

In Moroni 7, the great prophet Mormon provided what could be seen as a perfect parenting guide. The genius of the lecture is that he essentially described how the Lord goes about raising us, His children. What kind of a parent is the Lord? How does He bring us to Him? As we look at what Heavenly Father does, it might help us know what to do when we face parenting decisions. So let's look at four ways the Lord brings us to Him and see if we can use those principles to bring our children to Him as well.

Teach the children to discern between good and evil. Mormon began by talking about something that we deal with every day with kids: choosing the right. Specifically, how do we tell good from evil? On a daily basis, there are hundreds of choices to be made, even by the smallest child. Many of these choices are moral ones. Do I grab the doll from my sister? Do I lie to my mother? Do I sneak a pencil from the store? Do I cheat on my college entrance exam? Do I lie to my boss about missing work? Will I be faithful to my temple covenants? These decisions between good and evil form a continuum of choice that stretches from toddler-hood to our last breaths.

Mormon offered one magic key to help us with all of the choices. Here it is: "Wherefore, I show unto you the way to judge; for every thing which inviteth to do good, and to persuade to believe in Christ, is sent forth by the power and gift of Christ; wherefore ye may know with a perfect knowledge it is of God. But whatsoever thing persuadeth men to do evil, and believe not in Christ, and deny him, and serve not God, then ye may know with a perfect knowledge it is of the devil" (Moroni 7:16–17).

Let's talk about practical ways we might apply this advice. A good friend once told me that he doesn't hesitate during a television program or movie, when something is portrayed that is frankly evil (such as unfaithfulness, abuse, or any of the myriad sins that are regularly portrayed in the media as "normal" behavior), to speak up and say to his children, "Now, this is something we know as Latter-day Saints is wrong, and we don't agree with that." We can't turn off every show, but we can speak up and let our kids hear that this thing or that thing being portrayed is wrong. Talking often about the world around us can help children learn to distinguish good from evil.

We can also help children learn to listen to the Spirit. I taught seminary with a wonderful teacher named Brenda Smart, who would ask our teenagers at the beginning of each class, "How did you feel the Spirit yesterday?" or, "How were you guided by the Spirit?" At first, she received the blank stares that only teachers of teenagers can fully appreciate. But she kept asking and waiting, and pretty soon kids started sharing. The more they shared, the more they listened for the Spirit's promptings during the day. She was teaching them to discern between good and evil through the whisperings of the Spirit.

Exercise faith to bring miracles and the intervention of angels into their lives. Next, Mormon told us how to lay hold on every good thing in life by employing three great principles of power. We'd be cheating our children if we didn't make sure that they have these sources of power in their lives: faith, hope, and charity. He started with faith.

We might think about faith as something less than knowledge—just the starting point of a testimony—but Mormon was talking about something greater. Christ created the world through the power of faith (that is, visualizing it so strongly that it came into being), and faith is the power He uses to bring us back to Him. Mormon then wrote that He sends angels to minister to us because other people (often our parents) exercise faith on our behalf. He said that if we aren't getting angels and miracles in our lives, it's not because they aren't out there; it's because we have stopped believing that we can really get that help. This is a great principle of power but also a frightening responsibility. Our faith in calling forth angels has another side; if we don't exercise faith, they might not come.

Remember my cousin Kay and her advice about replacing obsessive worrying with positive praying? Offering a prayer like, "I pray for angels to attend this child" can shift the attitude from one of fear to one of faith. As a parent, you can't do any good for a child when you are anguished or frantic; you only do damage. You have to get to a place of faith and peace to be inspired about how to help. There are legions of angels to help us.

Communicate, through word and deed, a firm hope in Christ in every situation. We can help our loved ones see the big picture because we see it. Here's what Mormon said about hope: "And again, my beloved brethren, I would speak unto you concerning hope. How is it that ye can attain unto faith, save ye shall have hope? And what is it that ye shall hope for? Behold I say unto you that ye shall have hope through the atonement of Christ and the power of his resurrection, to be raised unto life eternal, and this because of your faith in him according to the promise" (Moroni 7:40–41).

What does hope have to do with parenting? Well, it has everything to do with the atmosphere in the home because a hopeful parent sees the bright side. When your little children are afraid, you are brave. When your grown children call with problems, you are full of encouragement. When there is illness, death, or sin, you are the one to point the family toward the hope the Savior offers. Your children hear you say, often, that you know things will work out, that you have faith in them, that you believe in them. Hope is, as Emily Dickinson said, "the song without the words that never stops" in the heart.[1]

President Boyd K. Packer told a story about a time when his wife went to the mortuary to help a young family who had lost a little boy. She found a scene of complete despair—there lay the beloved little boy in his coffin, and his grief-stricken mother could not bear to close the lid. Sister Packer noticed that the little boy's blanket had been placed nearby, and she took the blanket and said to the mother, 'Here, let's get him tucked in." Together, they tucked the blanket around him, up under his chin, and suddenly he looked just like he was going to sleep. The mother was then able to leave, and the Savior's words came to mind, "[He] is not dead, but only sleepeth" (Matthew 9:24). In a quiet, grandmotherly way, Sister Packer brought the hope of the resurrection to that grieving mother.[2]

Pray for pure Christlike love—to see the child as Christ does. Finally, Mormon got to the center of parenting: love, or charity, as it is called in the scriptures. "But charity is the pure love of Christ, and it endureth forever; and whoso is found possessed of it at the last day, it shall be well with him. Wherefore, my beloved brethren, pray unto the Father with all the energy of heart, that ye may be filled with this love, which he hath bestowed upon all who are true followers of his Son, Jesus Christ" (Moroni 7:47–48).

Every one of us (at least those of us who are in touch with reality) has trouble loving our kids at times. Some children are difficult to love, and most have stages when it would be much easier just to shoot them and do baptisms for the dead later! We're given these challenges, I think, so that we will understand how far God condescends to love us. He expects us to pray to Him to help us love our children the way He does.

If you will pray every day to feel about your children or grand-children the way Christ and Heavenly Father do, it may significantly change your relationship with them. One mother who was praying daily to love a difficult teenager was surprised when a strong impression came to her that she should smile more at this boy. That was it—just smile more. So she started consciously reminding herself to smile at him when he came into a room, when she was talking to him, and when they were driving together—a special challenge with boys. Years later, she was surprised when he wrote her from the mission field. "Dear Mom, I've never thanked you for smiling at me so much. You always seemed so happy to see me, and I often felt so bad about myself during those high school years that your smiling face meant more than you will ever know."

Ironically, sometimes loving more means getting tougher. A great lesson we learn from Alcoholics Anonymous is the principle of enabling. That is, we often collude in the destruction of those we love by enabling them to avoid the consequences of bad behavior. We bail out the drinking or drug-addicted child, allow the lazy one to live at home and not work, or encourage the rebellious one by laughing off disobedience.

As we pray to love our children the way God loves them, we may become tougher when we need to be without being angry or vindictive. Also, we may be blessed with a longer vision of the rebellious child, helping us see past current behavior to good behavior beyond. When we see the child as God sees him or her, we may have the courage to reprove with sharpness and at other times overlook the weakness and emphasize all there is to love in that child. Only Christ can guide us in this.

Love means that we learn to accept the children we have—not the ones we imagined we would have—and we embrace them, faults and all. This is a great lesson we may spend a lifetime learning. Along the way, we're never alone. God and angels stand at the ready to help us from worlds unseen.

There are thousands of books written about parenting, but this one sermon by Mormon may be the most important text available on the subject. Following these four steps as we raise our children will help to make their lives happier, and the world a better place for their being in it.

From Guilty to Grateful: When Ye Shall Receive These Things (Moroni 10)

When we think of the sacrifices that every contributor, from Nephi to Moroni, made to create this record, and then think about what Joseph Smith went through to translate, transcribe, and publish it, we should be filled with wonder at this miracle of a book. Why then does it seem so hard to pick up that book lying on the nightstand and actually read it every day? Let's examine a few reasons about why it seems so difficult to make scripture study a part of our daily routines.

Guilty or Grateful?

One reason it's hard to pick up the scriptures may be that the scriptures remind us of our shortcomings. Nobody likes feeling guilty, and it's human nature to avoid it if we possibly can. We may not admit to ourselves that we avoid the scriptures because they make us feel guilty, but guilt may be lurking in the background as we make the decision about whether to open them up each day. We really don't want to hear about one more thing we aren't doing!

But the central purpose of the scriptures is not to make us feel guilty. Moroni suggested what he thought we should feel when we read them: "Behold, I would exhort you that when ye shall read these things, if it be wisdom in God that ye should read them, that ye would remember how merciful the Lord hath been unto the children of men, from the creation of Adam even down until the time that ye shall receive these things, and ponder it in your hearts" (Moroni 10:3).

Moroni's comments remind us that we may have a wrong notion of the real purpose of the scriptures and that we should be feeling grateful when we pick them up. The purpose of the scriptures isn't primarily to make us feel guilty, though that may happen at times. It isn't just to tell us stories or even to give us a set of rules that will save us. The purpose of the scriptures is to teach us about Jesus Christ and His dealings with all of His children. Just as the Liahona functioned as a guide to food and water, the purpose of the scriptures is to lead us to Christ, the source of life eternal. The result of each scriptural encounter should be that Jesus comes more fully into our daily lives, that we might have a little more power to live as He would have us live.

The Scriptures Don't Save Us

The Jews of Jesus's day had such a reverence for God's word that they believed salvation was to be found in the scriptures themselves. In response to that idea, Jesus said, "Search the scriptures; for in them ye think ye have eternal life: and they are they which testify of me" (John 5:39). In other words, search the scriptures because even though you think the word will save you, it won't, and they will tell you so. The scriptures are only there to lead you to Christ. The scriptures don't save us; Christ saves us, the scriptures are simply there to point to Him. As Nephi found in his hunting adventures, the Liahona wasn't dinner—it just provided the directions for finding the food.

To employ another metaphor, the scriptures are the vehicle that helps us to travel toward salvation, but Jesus is the destination. Spending all of your time focusing on the rules and regulations that are listed in the scriptures is like living in your car when a glorious palace awaits you at the end of the road. As long as you understand its purpose, a car is quite helpful when you have a long journey ahead, but it isn't suitable as a residence. We need to use the scriptures as they are intended—as a vehicle that takes us toward Christ.

How will shifting the emphasis onto Jesus change our feelings toward scripture study? Well, the wonderful thing about any encounter with the Savior is this: Even though we invariably emerge with a greater understanding of our own unworthiness, we also emerge with an even greater appreciation of His grace and mercy and a "lively hope" in His power to save us (1 Peter 1:3). Guilt may be there, but when we seek Jesus through the scriptures, we are filled with hope.

C. S. Lewis expresses it thus: "[To have faith in Christ] means, of course, trying to do all that He says. . . . But trying in a new way, a less worried way. Not doing these things in order to be saved, but because He has begun to save you already. Not hoping to get to Heaven as a reward for your actions, but inevitably wanting to act in a certain way because a first faint gleam of Heaven is already inside you."[3]

Getting to Know Him

And that is what matters about the scriptures—not that we know them better than our neighbors, but that through them we come to know Him. It matters little how we wade into the scriptures, whether through the historical context, the doctrines, the literary devices, or the symbolic meanings. What matters is that we get to the center: the connection to the Savior. If we stop before we get to that final life-changing step, then we come away with a laundry list of "should-dos" rather than a glorious vision of "can-dos."

Approaching the Book of Mormon as a testament of Christ is the best way to really appreciate its power, feel its comfort, and benefit from its unique wisdom. Its purpose is consistent throughout. Here's the testimony of its first contributor, the brilliant, brave hero Nephi: "And now behold, I say unto you that the right way is to believe in Christ, and deny him not; and Christ is the Holy One of Israel; wherefore ye must bow down before him, and worship him with all your might, mind, and strength, and your whole soul; and if ye do this ye shall in nowise be cast out" (2 Nephi 25:29).

And now the testimony of the final contributor, the equally brilliant and brave hero Moroni: "And again, if ye by the grace of God are perfect in Christ, and deny not his power, then are ye sanctified in Christ by the grace of God, through the shedding of the blood of Christ, which is in the covenant of the Father unto the remission of your sins, that ye become holy, without spot" (Moroni 10:33).

Last of all, I add my humble witness that there is divine inspiration in the Book of Mormon. Its stories and sermons are applicable to our modern problems, and its message is more modern than any technology; it is timeless. Start to finish, the Book of Mormon is a testament of Christ, and as we allow its message to sink into our hearts, we will find new ways to invite Him into our hearts and our homes.

Notes

1. Emily Dickinson, "Hope Is the Thing with Feathers," *Emily Dickinson, Selected Poems* (New York: Random House, 2000).

2. Boyd K. Packer, *The Holy Temple* (Salt Lake City: Bookcraft, 1980).

3. C. S. Lewis, "What Christians Want to Know," *Mere Christianity*, (New York: HarperCollins, 1952).

Your Stories and Thoughts

Conclusion: Prophet or Loss? How We Feel about Joseph Smith Now

"When I was a child, I spake as a child, I understood as a child, I thought as a child: but when I became a man, I put away childish things" (1 Corinthians 13:11).

When I was growing up, I knew two basic things about Joseph Smith. First, he was a prophet—the most important prophet in history. I could quote (or at least paraphrase) John Taylor's famous assertion that Joseph Smith had done more for the salvation of the world than any other man, save Christ only (see D&C 135:3). By extension, I felt that he was nearly perfect, and the stories about him always centered on his Christlike qualities. Second, I knew that not many people understood the greatness of Joseph Smith—that ever since he received his remarkable First Vision, people had been persecuting him. Biographies about the Prophet Joseph fell into two categories: those by faithful members who praised his accomplishments and accepted the divine origin of his revelations and those by enemies of the Church who tried to expose him as a fraud. Faithful members embraced the first documents and avoided the others.

This was an easier world—them against us. However, over the last several decades, the general thrust of scholarship in regards to historical figures has been full disclosure, warts and all. And with the 2005 publication of the monumental work *Joseph Smith: Rough Stone Rolling*

The User-Friendly Book of Mormon

by Richard Bushman, a larger portion of the Church membership is coming to understand that the truth about Joseph Smith. Like the truth about every human being, he lies somewhere between the sentimental portraits of him as a saintly being and the angry portrayals of him as a scoundrel.

For example, Bushman wrote that Joseph Smith, not Brigham Young, was the original polygamist. He married and had intimate relations with several women and was sealed to many more after his death. This fact has come as a surprise to many Latter-day Saints. Many of the persecutions heaped upon Joseph were directly connected to this practice rather than specifically to his religious beliefs. He also had quite a temper, tended to displays of vanity, and recorded at least eleven versions of his First Vision before putting forward the official version we have today in the scriptures. He did not translate the Book of Mormon quite in the way the illustrations depict; instead, he was often looking into a seerstone (sometimes nestled in his hat) rather than at the plates.

And so it continues. The Martyrdom becomes a different story: rather than just an angry mob with no provocation other than hatred, we see Joseph ordering the destruction of the printing press of a local newspaper that opposed him, a crime for which he surrendered himself to the authorities at Carthage, where he was later killed by said mob. As Americans, we have strong feelings about the right to free speech, so this is disquieting.

After all of these disturbing revelations, the final shock to many members is this: instead of angrily tossing Bushman's carefully researched tome onto the heap of books that denigrate the Prophet Joseph, the leaders of the Church praised it as a truthful account of his life. What happened to the Prophet? In the last decade, I've heard the same two questions many times over. First, a thoughtful member asks, "Did you read *Rough Stone Rolling*?" When I say yes, the next question is simply, "Well, what do you think?"

Think is the operative word here. We're having, perhaps for the first time, to think hard about Joseph Smith. He isn't an easy think, either. On the one hand, our whole religion is built on Joseph Smith's revelations. On the other hand, a close look at his life tends to reveal that his behavior was, on many occasions, hard to explain. So what do you think? To accept Joseph Smith as a prophet, do you have to stop thinking and just accept him as a prophet? How do we reconcile what we now know about Joseph Smith with the way we viewed him twenty years ago?

What Do We Expect from a Prophet?

Here's where I would write the easy answer, if I could. But when it comes to questions that involve faith, the best we may sometimes hope for is to arrive at a better statement of the question. Most of us have read the Old Testament or are at least familiar with the life histories of the ancient prophets. The Jews were masters of the "warts and all" biography. In fact, they seemed to relish recounting embarrassing and even downright wicked moments from the lives of their greatest prophets.

For example, Noah got drunk and was seduced by his daughter-in-laws. Jacob cheated Esau out of a birthright under his mother's guidance. Elisha conjured up a bear to devour a little group of hooligans who were mocking him. The list goes on. The Jews had no problem understanding that their prophets were flawed individuals—in some cases (such as Saul and Sampson) tragically so—and yet they had unshakable faith that God worked through and inspired them. We know that the accounts recorded in the Old Testament began as oral histories, told and retold through the generations. So why keep all that bad stuff? Why not edit them to better inspire believers? Wouldn't we all be happier if our prophets were practically perfect?

It may be that, in the end, we feel betrayed—not so much by any thing that Joseph Smith did, but instead by what we were taught to expect of him. Hounded and persecuted by enemies, the early Latter-day Saint leaders felt no desire to expose the weaknesses of their leaders; there were plenty of people interested in doing that. Instead, the primary need was to circle the wagons and stay united as a people. Over time, the LDS Church has moved from being regarded as a cult to a gradual (though grudging) acceptance by the world as a legitimate religion. And, at the same time, modern scholarly research has shown Joseph Smith as a little less than the saintly being we revered to more of a charismatic prophet of Old Testament dimensions. For generations, we as a people were not willing to expose the faults of our own leaders, so this first, idealized view of Joseph Smith became for many of us part and parcel of our faith in his divine revelations. Can we accept that a man with flaws in his character could've also been divinely inspired?

The Witness of One Who Knew Him Well

I can, and I do. When I was in college, I became really interested in Joseph Smith, for I felt a personal connection to him. My grandmother, Veda Jane Walker Green, lost her mother at the age of five and was raised by her grandmother, Mary Jane Shadden Walker. Mary Jane's aunt was Lucy Walker, Joseph Smith's fifth polygamous wife, who, later in life, often came to stay with Mary Jane and my grandma. These people were as real to my grandma as my grandma was to me. Polygamy, outlawed in 1890, was not a source of embarrassment to them as it is to us. For them, it was a principle, a part of their gospel faith.

The John Walker family left Connecticut and emigrated west in 1841. With colossal bad timing, they reached the town of Shoal Creek, just five miles from Haun's Mill, on the day the famous massacre occurred. John was shot in the arm and hid in the woods for two weeks. Eventually, his family found him and reached Nauvoo. But in Nauvoo, his wife, Lydia, and several of the children became ill, and eventually Lydia died in January of 1842. Exhausted with grief and in ill health, John Walker was sent by the Prophet on a "mission" to a place with a healthier climate to recover his strength. The Prophet Joseph and his wife took the older children in the family into the Mansion House in Nauvoo, and other families invited the remaining children to stay with them. Later that year, Joseph proposed a polygamous marriage to Lucy. Only eighteen years old, she looked to Joseph as a second father. She was horrified and repulsed and told him so. Here's her account of the experience:

> In the year of 1842 President Joseph Smith sought an interview with me, and said; "I have a message for you. I have been commanded of God to take another wife, and you are the woman." My astonishment knew no bounds. This announcement was indeed a thunderbolt to me. He asked me if I believed him to be a prophet of God. "Most assuredly I do," I replied. He fully explained to me the principle of plural or celestial marriage. Said this principle was again to be restored for the benefit of the human family. That it would prove an everlasting blessing to my father's house, and form a chain that could never be broken,

worlds without end. "What have you to say?" he asked. "Nothing. How could I speak, or what could I say?" He said, "If you will pray sincerely for light and understanding in relation thereto, you shall receive a testimony of the correctness of the principle."

I thought I prayed sincerely, but was so unwilling to consider the matter favorably that I fear I did not ask in faith for light. Gross darkness instead of light took possession of my mind. I was tempted and tortured beyond endurance until life was not desirable. Oh that the grave would kindly receive me, that I might find rest on the bosom of my dear mother. Why should I be chosen from among Thy daughters, Father, I am only a child in years and experience. No mother to counsel; no father near to tell me what to do in this trying hour. Oh, let this bitter cup pass. And thus I prayed in the agony of my soul.

The Prophet discerned my sorrow. He saw how unhappy I was, and sought an opportunity of again speaking to me on this subject, and said: "Although I cannot, under existing circumstances acknowledge you as my wife, the time is near when we will go beyond the Rocky Mountains and then you will be acknowledged and honored as my wife." He also said, "This principle will yet be believed and practiced by the righteous. I have no flattering words to offer. It is a command of God to you. I will give you until tomorrow to decide this matter. If you reject this message the gate will be closed forever against you."

At this point, Lucy responded in a way that makes me proud to be her descendant. I imagine this tiny eighteen-year-old girl, facing the man who was God's mouthpiece on earth and demanding her right to be guided by the Spirit.

· This aroused every drop of Scotch in my veins. For a few moments I stood fearless before him, and looked him in the eye. I felt at this moment that I was called to place myself upon the altar a living sacrifice—perhaps to brook the world in disgrace and incur the displeasure and contempt of my youthful companions; all my dreams of happiness blown to the four winds. This was too much, for as yet no shadow had crossed my path, aside from the death of my dear mother. The future to me had been one bright, cloudless day. I had been speechless, but at last found utterance and said, "Although you are a prophet of God you could not induce me to take a step of so great importance, unless I knew that God approved my course. I would rather die. I have tried to pray but received no comfort, no light," and emphatically forbade him speaking to me again on the subject. Every feeling of my soul revolted against it. Said I, "The same God who has sent this message is the Being I have worshipped from my early childhood and He must manifest His will to me." He walked across the room, returned and stood before me with the most beautiful expression of countenance, and said: "God Almighty bless you. You shall have the manifestation of the will of God concerning you; a testimony that you can never deny. I will tell what it will be. It shall be that joy and peace that you never knew."

Oh, how earnestly I prayed for these words to be fulfilled. It was near dawn after another sleepless night when my room was lighted up by a heavenly influence. To me it was, in comparison, like the brilliant sun shining through the darkest cloud. The words of the Prophet were indeed fulfilled. My soul was filled with a calm, sweet peace that "I never knew." Supreme happiness took possession of me, and I received a powerful and irresistible testimony of the truth of plural marriage, which has been like an anchor to the soul through all the trials of life. I felt that I must go out in to the morning air and give vent to the joy and gratitude that filled my soul. As I descended the stairs, President Smith opened the door below, took me by the hand and said: "Thank God, you have the testimony, I too have prayed." He led me to a chair, placed his hands upon my head, and blessed me with every blessing my heart could possibly desire.[1]

In Her Own Hand

I remember going to the Church Archives and finding this account, written in Lucy's own hand. As I copied it into my notebook, I felt something coming to me across the century that separated our lives, and that something was Lucy's conviction that Joseph Smith was a prophet. To the end of her life, Lucy was faithful to that conviction. When she was an old lady, Joseph F. Smith, then president of the Church, took her on a tour of the Primary organizations in Idaho. She told the children about her experiences with the Prophet, and President Joseph F. Smith invited the children to come up and shake her hand and receive her blessing as the last living wife of Joseph Smith. This strong, stubborn Scottish girl believed that God had reached out to the world through Joseph Smith, and I suppose she knew him better than I ever will.

My Own Witness

Lucy's witness is powerful, but we cannot live on borrowed light. I can't be faithful to Joseph Smith just because my ancestors believed in his mission. One night, as I was in the midst of researching Lucy's life, I opened the *Lectures on Faith*, which is a collection of transcripts of the lessons Joseph taught in the School of the Prophets in Nauvoo. At the end of this little book is something called the "King Follett Discourse." It's actually a funeral address for a fellow named King Follett, delivered just a short time before Joseph's own death in Carthage, and it is an important document in our history.

As I read, I began to see Joseph Smith in a new way. At the beginning of the speech, he comes across as weary, angry, and almost paranoid about his enemies. At points in the speech, he seemed near hysteria, and from the narrative it is clear that this was an awful time for him. Yet as he warmed to his subject, his emotions seemed to even out, and the inspiration began to flow. I hadn't realized until this reading how many fundamental doctrines of the Church—life-changing, reality bending doctrines such as the nature of our eternal personalities, the nature of God, the eternal nature of families, and the divine origin of man—are taught in this one place.

I was completely transfixed by what I was reading. I felt as though I were there in the congregation and could see him with his harried, hounded expression, yet lit up by an inner light that at times must have been a mystery even to himself. Suddenly, I realized that I was no longer seated at my desk but was standing in the middle of the reading room, and a few people were staring at me. Without realizing it, I had risen to my feet. It was impossible to sit anymore, so I began to walk. It was all I could do not to shout out loud! I felt like I had stumbled upon a gold mine in my own backyard. I couldn't believe my luck; I held a priceless treasure of truth in my hands, and I felt blessed beyond measure to have it.

From that moment over forty years ago to this one, I have believed that Joseph Smith was inspired and directed by God to restore precious truths to the earth. I've also believed that God used both Joseph's strengths *and* flaws in his nature to accomplish this task, because God needed somebody who could think way outside the box. Like my

Aunt Lucy, this conviction came to me unexpectedly and undeniably. I admit that I'm still occasionally troubled by parts of Joseph's life. But I understand from my own life that the bare facts about me don't always tell the whole truth. I am sure I would not like all the embarrassing details of my life to be carefully recorded, dissected, and discussed. But I'd hope that, even if they were, the truth of my life is manifest by the bulk of my actions rather than by my mistakes. I'm not 100 percent comfortable with all the facts of Joseph Smith's life, but I am thankful for the truth of it, and I know God used him to change the world.

What I Expect and What I Accept

So even though the Prophet Joseph Smith has turned out to be different than I expected, I am unwilling to abandon my faith in his prophetic mission. I have a lot to lose if I give up on Joseph. If I give him up, I'd have to give up on eternal marriage, the promise of eternal families, and the divine origin of our personalities. I'd have to give up Alma 32 and Alma 7:11–13, passages that have taught me more about my relationship to the Savior than any fifty volumes of Bible commentary ever could. I'd have to give up the vision of Lehi, the life-changing teachings about faith and miracles in Mormon's account, and the infinitely touching moment when 2,500 people dropped to their knees and begged the Savior to stay with them just a little longer. I'd have to give up the Book of Mormon. I'm not willing to do that. It's meant too much to my spiritual life to part with it.

If I give up on Joseph Smith, I'd have to give up a part of who I am. My life has been guided by the positive theology he taught. My behavior has been shaped by my covenants—especially the covenants I made in the temple—of fidelity, chastity, obedience, sacrifice, and general good behavior. I'd have to give up being sealed to my husband and family, a fact that brings me daily joy and comfort. Even my health would be affected, for it is a result not only my own adherence to the Word of Wisdom but also of my forbearers' adherence to that code of health. I'd have to give up on the idea that God is a wonderfully personal and direct and involved Being, an idea that seemed reasonable to people in other times but has become quite unfashionable in a world that worships science and movie stars. It's all just too much to give up.

So what do I expect from Joseph Smith? I don't know anymore. But I do know what I accept, and I know what is expected of me. I accept that God worked through the Prophet Joseph, and I know that I'm expected to pick up my end of the log and carry on the work he began. I accept that, like Lucy, I need to think for myself and question dogma that seems unreasonable to me. But my questioning will never take me so far that I deny that original moment when I felt a connection to the divine, just as he never denied his moments of inspiration.

It's so easy to deconstruct the greatness of an individual and as a result miss the forest for the trees. Joseph Smith was a religious genius, one of those characters who comes along rarely and changes the face of things. I'm lucky to enjoy the advantages that come with understanding his revelations. And so I stand with him, warts and all. With a grateful heart, I echo the words of Brigham Young,

> I honor and revere the name of Joseph Smith. I delight to hear it; I love it. I love his doctrine. . . . He took heaven, figuratively speaking, and brought it down to earth; and he took the earth, brought it up, and opened up, in plainness and simplicity, the things of God; and that is the beauty of his mission. . . . I feel like shouting Hallelujah, all the time, when I think that I ever knew Joseph Smith, the Prophet whom the Lord raised up and ordained, and to whom he gave keys and power to build up the Kingdom of God on earth and sustain it.[2]

Notes

1. See Rodney Wilson Walker and Noel C. Stevenson, *Ancestry and Descendants of John Walker*, https://archive.org/stream /ancestrydescenda00walk/ancestrydescenda00walk_djvu.txt.

2. Brigham Young, *Discourses of Brigham Young* (Salt Lake City, Deseret Book, 1951).

About the Author

Marilyn Green Faulkner likes to read and talk about books. She earned a BA in humanities and an MA in literature and sneaks away to Cambridge or Oxford University every summer for further study. For seven years, she wrote a monthly column on the classics for *Meridian Magazine*. Her first book, *Back to the Best Books: How the Classics Can Change Your Life*, was a finalist for nonfiction indie book of the year in 2010. As senior content creator for FMG Suite (a digital marketing company), she writes articles and videos on financial marketing.

Marilyn served an LDS mission in Japan, has been a presenter at the BYU Women's Conference, and speaks regularly at youth and Relief Society conferences. She currently teaches a weekly scripture class in the Del Mar California Stake. With her husband, Craig, she has five children, a growing group of grandchildren, and Frankie, the world's best dog. Find her at www.marilyngreenfaulkner.com.